Pedram Khosronejad (Ed.)

Untold Stories

Iranian Studies

edited by

Dr. Pedram Khosronejad
(University of St. Andrews)

Volume 2

LIT

UNTOLD STORIES

The socio-cultural life of images in Qajar Era Iran

edited by

Pedram Khosronejad

LIT

Cover image: © Golestan Palace Photo Archive, Iran

This publication is supported by
The Soudavar Memorial Foundation
The Houtan Foundation
Groupe Sociétés, Religions, Laïcités – CNRS

This book is printed on acid-free paper.

Bibliographic information published by the Deutsche Nationalbibliothek
The Deutsche Nationalbibliothek lists this publication in the Deutsche Nationalbibliografie; detailed bibliographic data are available in the Internet at http://dnb.d-nb.de.

ISBN 978-3-643-90607-6

A catalogue record for this book is available from the British Library

Klosbachstr. 107
CH-8032 Zürich
Tel. +41 (0) 44-251 75 05
Fax +41 (0) 44-251 75 06
E-Mail: zuerich@lit-verlag.ch
http://www.lit-verlag.ch

LIT VERLAG Dr. W. Hopf
Berlin 2015
Fresnostr. 2
D-48159 Münster
Tel. +49 (0) 2 51-62 03 20
Fax +49 (0) 2 51-23 19 72
E-Mail: lit@lit-verlag.de
http://www.lit-verlag.de

Distribution:
In the UK: Global Book Marketing, e-mail: mo@centralbooks.com
In North America: International Specialized Book Services, e-mail: orders@isbs.com
In Germany: LIT Verlag Fresnostr. 2, D-48159 Münster
Tel. +49 (0) 2 51-620 32 22, Fax +49 (0) 2 51-922 60 99,
E-mail: vertrieb@lit-verlag.de

In Austria: Medienlogistik Pichler-ÖBZ, e-mail: mlo@medien-logistik.at
e-books are available at www.litwebshop.de

In Memoriam:
Farrokh Ghafari (1921 – 2006)

Tracking a modern visual element through two similar conditions of chaos 117
Siamak Hajimohammad

Bibliography 141

Index 147

Foreword

In Iran, the history of photography and cinematography is mired with doubts and ambiguities. The first photographic apparatuses were given to the Iranian Qajar (1794-1925) monarch, Mohammad Shah (1808–1848), somewhere between 1839 and 1842, by the two colonial powers in Iran – Great Britain and Russia. Also, cinematography was introduced for the first time to another Qajar monarch, Mozafar al-Din Shah (1853–1907), at some time between 1899 and 1900. Taking this into account, it is clear that the Qajar kings were in great part responsible for the birth of photography and cinematography in Iran, and also that the development of these technologies was influenced by the personal tastes of these monarchs.

Whilst academic debates have focused on Qajar photography and cinematography from the viewpoint of historical analysis and technical aspects, there does not appear to be any anthropological, and in particular, visual anthropological research on these two important visual mediums. As a result of this simple but crucial observation, in 2011 (27-28 August) with the collaboration of *Prof. M. M. Eskandari-Qajar* (President, IQSA; Director, Middle East Studies Program, Santa Barbara City College, USA) we organised a conference and film program on Photography and Cinematography in Qajar Era Iran.

In this program, our aim was to encourage and invite scholars who are working in fields such as visual anthropology, ethnographical film, media and visual studies, and whose interests coincided with this symposium's, to present their work. During this two-day symposium and film season we discussed and developed ideas deriving from social and visual anthropological research, and discerned and debated the diverse types and aspects of photography and cinematography of the Qajar era in Iran, and not exclusively through monarchic art.

The following scholars made contributions to our program: Mirjam Brusius (Image problems: Photographic (self-)representations of Persia by

Nasser al-Din Shah and European Travelling Artists in the mid 19th Century, late Qajar Era), Layla Diba *(Qajar Photography and its Influence on Modern and Contemporary Persian Painting),* Alexander Fischer (Back in the Picture: the Search for Qajar-era Motion Pictures in Three Prominent European Film Archives), Alireza Ghasemkhan (Iran's Qajar Cinema and the First Steps towards Decanonization), Carmen Perez Gonzalez (The Written Image: Text and Nineteenth-Century Iranian Portrait Studio Photography), Elahe Helbig (The Eye of the Shah: Photographic Documentation of the Land and People of Persia by means of the Photo Album by Abdullah Qajar), Basak Kilerci (Portraiture in Qajar Iran and Ottoman Empire: A Comparative Approach), Ali Mir-Ansari *(The Comparative Social Impact of Theatre and Cinema in Iran: A Case Study of the Constitutional Era),* Hamid Naficy (Qajar Era Cinemas Mode of Production), Golbarg Rekabtalaei (*Picturing Modernity: Early Cinema in Qajar Era Iran), and* Corien J.M. Vuurman (*Persia Through the Lens of a Dutch Businessman: the Albert Hotz Collection of Nineteenth-century Photographs at the Leiden University Library in Netherlands).* That some of these studies are not included here in our collection is generally due to the author's own choice, the editor's decision, or because they were scheduled to appear elsewhere. Therefore only two of the presented papers of our program are included in our collection.

The main chapters of the present volume were made through a call for presentations for the above program among specialists of the field in Iran. Unfortunately, not all of our colleagues from Iran could participate in our program due to of visa issues; however, they submitted their papers for our program and this volume is largely comprised of these submitted papers. Therefore, the main objective of this book is to present the researches of Iranian specialists in Qajar photography and cinematography infrom the viewpoint of art history, visual history, social history and visual anthropology of the Qajar period of Iran.

I would like to thank all the contributors for an exceptionally good humoured during our program. My special thanks should go to Dr. H. Marashi, who translated most of the chapters of this book from Persian to English. I am also grateful for the financial support of the Soudavar Memorial Foundation, the Houtan Foundation and The International Qajar Studies Association, who were the main supporters of our program. I am also deeply grateful for the backing and collaboration of the Golestan Palace Photo Archive and all of its personnel for their constant support. Finally, without the help of my friend and colleague Mr. A. Ghasemkhan I could never have run such a fruitful program.

Here I wish to acknowledge that most of the pictures of this volume are from the Golestan Palace Photo Archive and Central Library of University of Tehran. We are grateful for its kind support.

P. Khosronejad
Visiting Professor
Institute of Advance Studies of Nantes
January 2015

Photographic documentation of *Taʿzieh* and *Taqlid* during the Qajar era

Ali Gholipoor

There is little (if any) doubt that *muqalids* (performers of comical plays) and *taʿzieh-khans* (performers of tragic religious plays better known as passion plays) were among the entertainers of the Qajar era who attracted a sizeable audience of fans and thus drew the lenses of photographers. The reason behind this claim is the multitude and diversity of such photos in the archives of Golestan Palace and other collections. The camera that was most appealing to both Nasser al-Din Shah and his son Mozafar al-Din Shah became an instrument to record a significant portion of the entertainments of their day and age.

Nasser al-Din Shah and Mozafar al-Din Shah were also especially interested in *Taqlid* and *Taʿzieh* or *shabih-khani* as the two forms of drama bore the potential to formulate Iranian theatre – an indigenous theatre which was the product of the evolution of traditional plays and Iranian rituals. Iranian theatre did not merge into existence in this way, however (Ghaffary 1984); rather, it established itself through the writing of screenplays in the European tradition, translating French dramas, establishing a theatre hall in Darolfonoon, and performing the translations on stage (Malekpoor 1984).

The emergence of screenplay-writing marked the beginning of Iranian theatre, a beginning that parted from the theatrical traditions of Iran such as *Taʿzieh* and *Taqlid* and put forth a new form of theatrical expression. By analyzing the nonverbal documents remaining from *Taʿzieh* and *Taqlid*, one can rediscover certain features of this forgotten and un-evolved theatre. This rediscovery may be pursued to seek the answer to this question: why do *muqalids* have a theatrical pose in photos from the era of Nasser al-Din Shah and Mozafar al-Din Shah while *taʿzieh-khans* do not?

Put more explicitly, why is it that *muqalids* appear in photos as if they are performing while *taʿzieh-khans* pose without theatrical expressions? This discrepancy between the two classes of Qajar era performers is vividly clear in one of the photographs of the Golestan Palace archives (fig. 1)

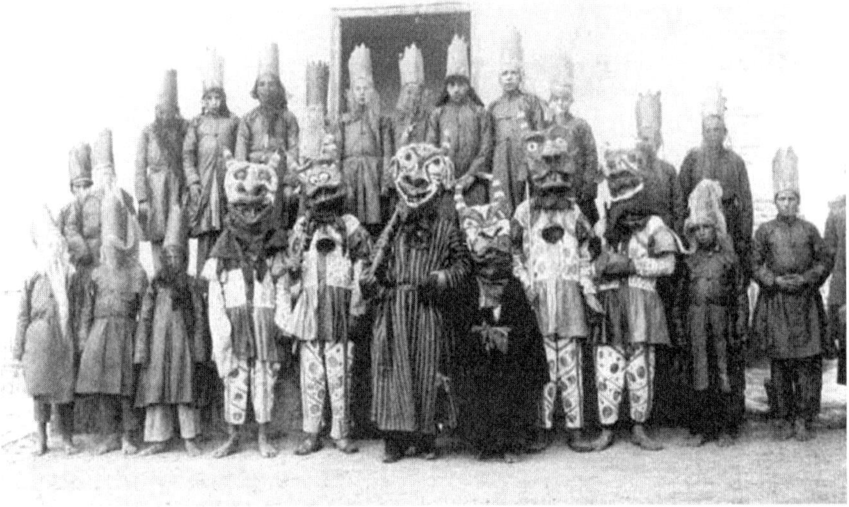

Figure 1: A group of Taʿzieh-khans: Hazrat-i Suleyman.

To further understand the photos of *muqalids* and *taʿzieh-khans*, one must elaborate the nature and essence of these forms of drama while also looking into some of the revived films of the Golestan archives. Two such films that bear significant importance are one that is very similar to a slapstick comedy and one in which Mozafar al-Din Shah and his entourage reconstruct a hunting scene.[1]

What the audience sees in these two films is the acting of a cast who have no knowledge of drama techniques. To begin, the actors never look at the camera in a slapstick and never laugh despite their comical and hyperbolical acts. They are trained actors who play their parts seriously and try

1 Zahedian 2004.

to make everyone laugh while pretending as if they are not conscious of the camera or audience (fig. 2)

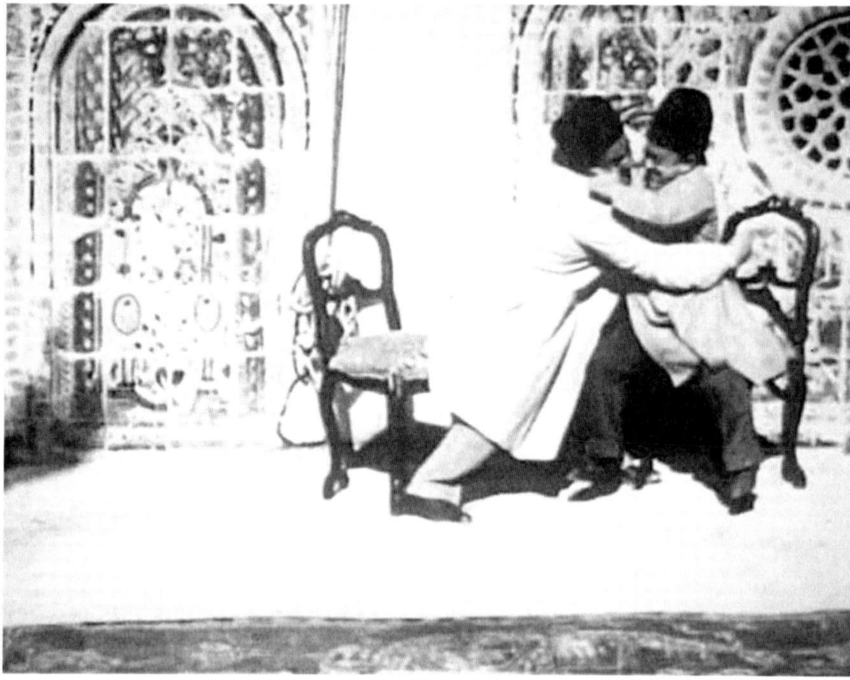

Figure 2: A scene from a comical play

In the scene in which Mozafar al-Din Shah and his entourage are reconstructing a hunt, acting takes almost another form, whereby exaggerated acts have decreased and some look into the camera while others laugh alongside Mozafar al-Din Shah; the presence of the camera and the audience is felt more distinctly (fig. 3).

Through not taking acting seriously, they – Mozafar al-Din Shah, particularly – play their parts as if they have built a gap between the roles and themselves. This is indeed what *ta'zieh-khans* do in their performance. The question, therefore, is the source of those *muqalids* and the entourage of the king for acting before the camera. What have they imitated and how did they demonstrate their similarity to something else? And, most impor-

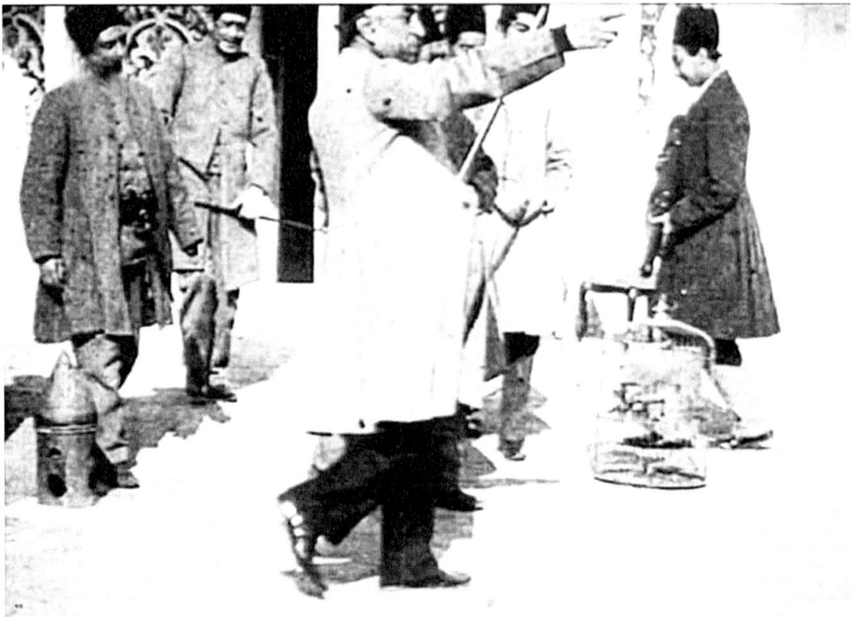

Figure 3: Mozafar al-Din Shah Shah and his entourage reconstructing a hunting scene.

tantly, how was *tashabuh*[2] conceived in the cultural context of the Qajar era performers?

Taʿzieh, Tashaboh, Taqlid and Hyperbole

Shabih-khani is another term for *taʿzieh*, which is the theatrization of what happened to the third Shiite Imam Hoseyn and his family in Karbala. This process consists of two founding elements: the content of the *taʿzieh*, which is the *ʿAshura* event, and the theatrization of the event, which is the specific form. The term *shabih*, which translates to 'impersonation' or 'likeness', falls between these two elements in that *taʿzieh* is theatrizing a likeness of what happened in Karbala and connotatively bears an emphasis on its being unrealistic.

The Iranian plays of the Qajar era carry a message in their titles, which to a certain extent portrays their structures. Generally speaking, different

[2] A key concept in this paper, which means the similarity of one thing to another.

kinds of puppet theatres – some of which use marionettes and ventriloquists and others a bald character – exist in the theatrical tradition of Iran, and the titles of these comedies signify a defiance of moral norms. The Farsi suffix used for this class of drama is *bazi*, which literally means 'play' and 'game' (*khaymihshab-bazi, luwbat-bazi, kachalak-bazi*); both in form and content, they are the opposite of the dramas which bear the Farsi suffix *khani*, which, in turn, means 'reading' (*taʿzieh-khani, shabih-khani, pardih-khani, surat-khani*[3], etc.). The suffix *bazi*, which meant that these were theatrizations, was apparently indicative of entertainment, facetiousness and *taqlid*, or imitation[4]. Hence, it becomes clear why *taʿzieh* was not named *shabih-bazi* but *shabih-khani.*

The theatrization of the Karbala event is a product of the Qajar era (Calmard 1996). Prior to that period, it was common for mourners to hold a procession. Despite this theatrization, the work of *shabih-khans* who performed *taʿzieh* was fundamentally in contrast to that of other actors engaged in *bazi*, as described above (Beeman & Ghaffari 2005, pp. 55–57). Hence, one very rarely finds a photo from the Qajar era that depicts a *taʿzieh-khan* in a theatrical pose. The only striking difference between the actors in such photos and politicians, princes, and other non-actors is their costumes – the actors resemble a choir group rather than actors (fig. 4). Even the very rare photos with a theatrical pose depict the actors in a highly urbane and graceful manner, with the maximum gesture being the point of a finger (fig. 5). The reason for this nontheatrical pose can be understood by elucidating the relationship between *tashabuh* and *taʿzieh*

In the words of Baktash (1979), the process undertaken by *taʿzieh* was in essence demonstrative of the principle of *tashabuh*, as the latter played a decisive role in the evolution and promotion of the former in a culture in which *taʿzieh* already was established. *Tashabuh* is a controversial concept in the evolution of *taʿzieh*; the controversy arises from the interpretation of certain Quranic verses by different theologians and clerics, whereby the simulation

---

3 The performer in *pardih-khani* and *surat-khani* stands in front of a curtain with religious paintings and narrates epic and religious stories.

4 *Taqlid* also means the similarity of one thing to another, just like *tashabuh*; yet it has a negative connotation.

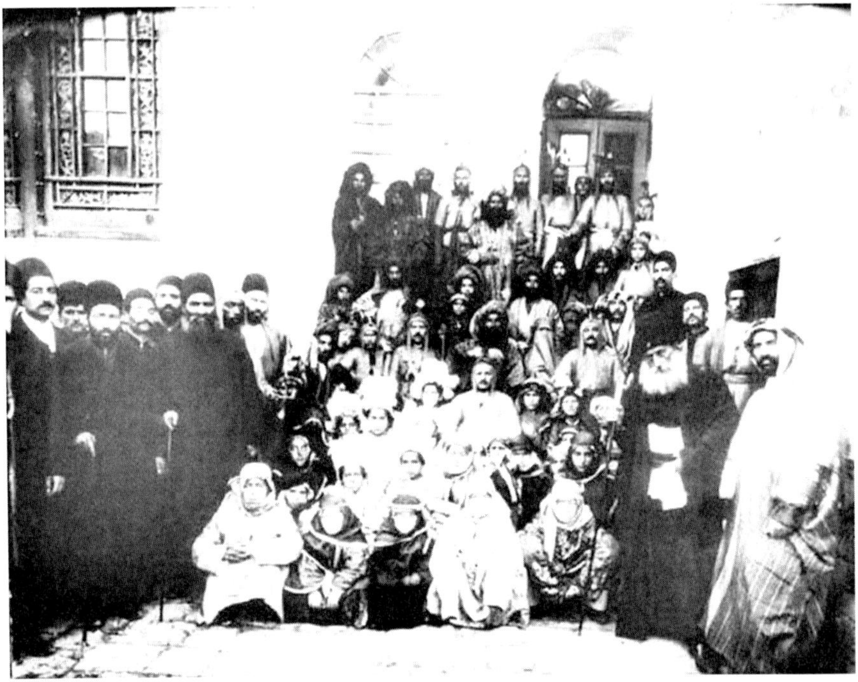

Figure 4: A group of Ta'zieh-khans.

of God to his creatures has been denounced[5]. *Tashabuh* established an opportunity in *ta'zieh* for identifying oneself with the character of the imams and also the sacred. This identification was founded upon the saying of the Prophet, 'anyone who assimilates oneself with a group is within that group'. Hence, *tashabuh* to the imams turned into an acceptable and appropriate act. Apparently, the majority of the Qajar era clerics who did not consider *tashabuh* in *ta'zieh* as *haram*, or forbidden, referred to the above saying for their argument. Had they not done so, Iranians likely would have had neither *ta'zieh* nor narrative religious paintings (Chelkowski 1989, p. 104). With the *fatwa* of the clerics allowing *ta'zieh*, both *ta'zieh* and narrative re-

5 Two verses of the Quran are most commonly referred to regarding this discussion. *'Ashura* (42), 11: ... There is nothing whatever like unto him... al-Ikhlas (112), 4: And there is none like unto Him.

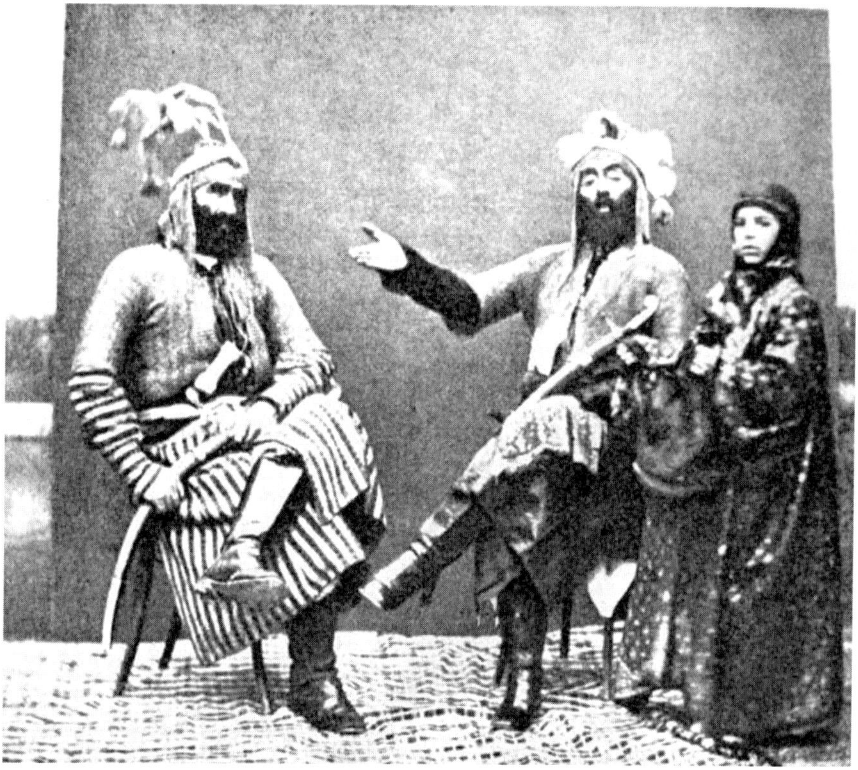

Figure 5: A group of Shabih-khans.

ligious paintings – which Peterson (Chelkowski 1989, p. 75) defines as the translation of *taʿzieh* into visual arts – rose to prominence in the Qajar era.

Yet, this important point should not be overlooked: *taʿzieh* and *shabih-khani* in the Qajar era were never considered forms of theatre but rather somewhere between rituals and theatre (Beeman & Ghaffari 2005, p. 51). In principle, many clerics and intellectuals did not define *taʿzieh* as theatre. Akhunzadeh (1970, p. 27), for example, considers *taʿzieh* disharmonious with reality and discordant with human nature – that is, neither realistic nor naturalistic. Orientologists who had seen dozens of theatrical performances in their own countries and were quite acquainted with theatrical conventions and skills of drama as well as *taʿzieh* have rightly distinguished the performances of *shabih-khans* and those of actors on stage in the Occident.

In their eyes, the most important task of *shabih-khans* was to provoke the audience to grief and make them shed tears; they did this while being incognizant of the skills and techniques of theatrical performance. Chodzko (1878), Pelly (1879), and Gobineau (1866), who conducted comparative studies of *taʿzieh* and Western theatre and who considered Iranians as possessing drama, visual arts and dramatic literature, emphasized the discrepancies between *shabih-khani* and performing in theatre.

Taʿzieh performers were regarded by clerics as mere *shabih-khans*, not actors; they were viewed as those who sing the story of Karbala written in poetry, an act not quintessentially different from that in which those singing elegies would engage (Aghaie 2005, pp. 375–6). Accordingly, the fear of and attempts to prevent the transformation of *taʿzieh* into theatre in the Qajar era have been clearly narrated by Hedayat (1960, p. 788); he writes that Westerners regard *taʿzieh* as being akin to their own theatre and entertainment, and that this conceptualization was extremely troublesome for the Shiite clerics of the day. He further notes the premonition of such a notion leading to rebellious confrontations by Moslems. Another example was Ali Muhammad Fakhimodowleh, who wrote that *taʿzieh* and elegies must not turn into Western-style theatres (cited by Shahidi 2001, p. 147).

In their perspective, the term 'theatre' suggested mere imitation and plays that were in defiance of morality; in other words, it was *taqlid* that during the Qajar years gradually found its way into *taʿzieh* and caused concern among the religious.[6] As *tashabuh* was the major component of *taʿzieh*, hyperbole served as the founding pillar of *taqlid*. In the latter, sexual humour best restricted to private life would be expressed bluntly in the public domain; this was often the theme of *taqlids*. The joke that Karim the Junkie – the most prominent of Nasser al-Din Shah's clowns – made with the private part of one of the performers of *taqlid* illustrates this issue most clearly (fig. 6). The question here is whether the photos of *muqalids* actually defied the norms and conventions of time, just as the semi-nude photos taken by Nasser al-Din Shah of his harem's women did. In effect, did the

6 *Taʿziyih muzhik*, or ridicule *taʿzieh* aggravated this concern more than anything else. Some view this structure of *taʿzieh* and nonreligious performance as the fountainheads of the formation of Iranian theater (Anvar 2005, p. 65).

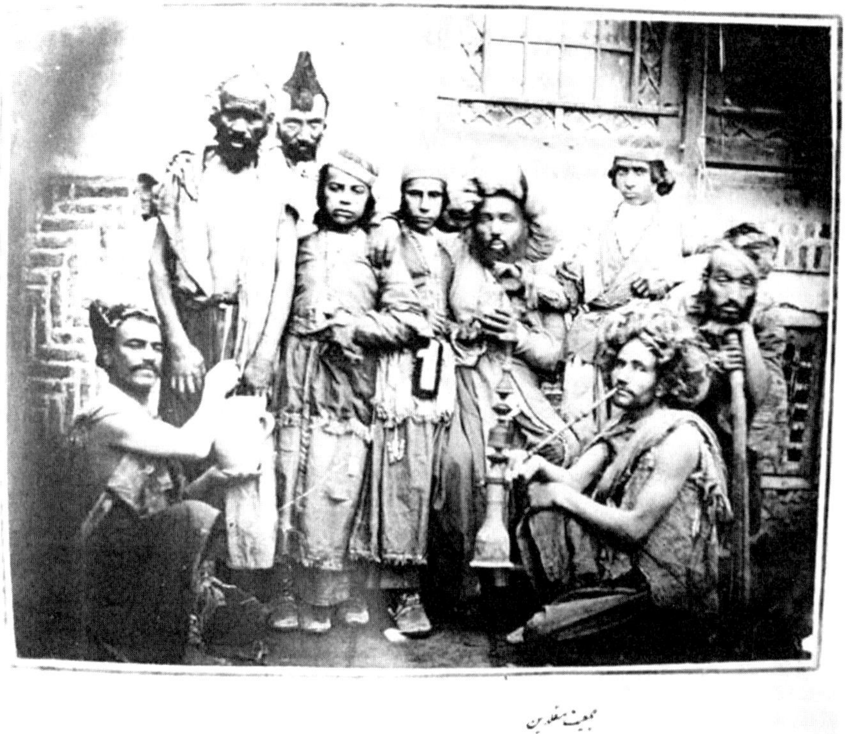

Figure 6: Karim the Junkie (seated in left) and his fellow acting company

religious climate of Iran during the Qajar dynasty embrace the pose of this *muqalid* (fig. 7)?

In his field studies of Iranian comical plays that have roots in the Qajar era, Beeman (1981, p. 521) illustrates the three inherent specificities of these plays within the cultural context of the time: sight gag, sexual humour and mocking of authority. He further refers to the jokes of Karim the Junkie compiled by Nurbakhsh (1976) and argues that if the texts of these jokes were juxtaposed with the photos and films, the conclusion would be that the performers of *taqlid* employed a theatrical system through which ragged looks and sexual humour were the principle techniques – and thus violated the norms of the religious society of the time. The body of the *muqalid* was a symbol of his profession, just as holding a pen in one's hand

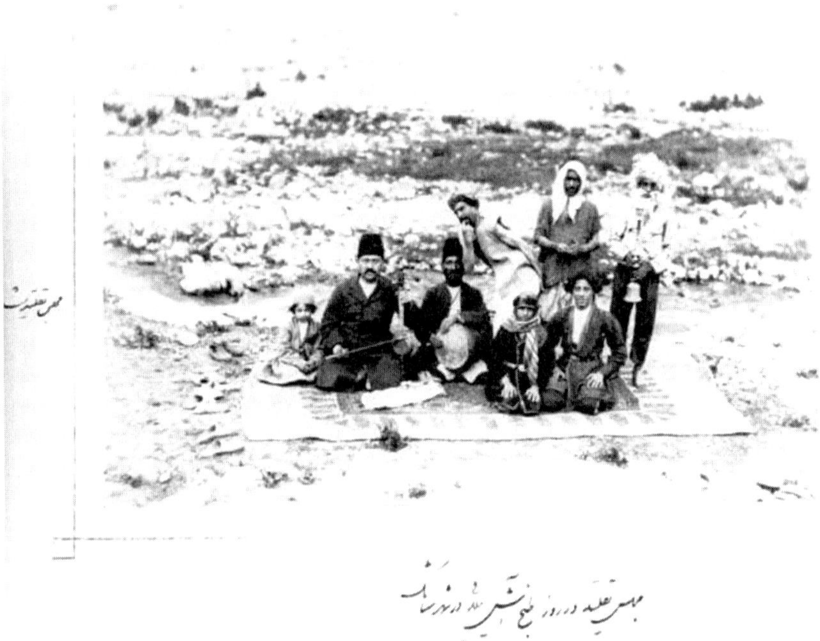

Figure 7: Group of muqalids who had accompanied Nasser al-Din Shah in a royal summer residence.

in Qajar era photos indicated a writer (fig. 8). The *muqalid*'s ragged look is the first and foremost symbol of his occupation of making people laugh with his body and looks and through sight gag (fig. 9).

Taqlid defined no border between laughing and provoking laughter. *Muqalids* would even pull the moustaches of their playmates when taking a photo alongside the shah, portraying a symbol of their profession (fig. 10). This was in direct contrast to the approach taken in *taʿzieh* – a nontheatrical performance to make people cry, i.e., exactly what hardline clerics wanted[7].

Many clerics who enjoyed considerable power and authority during the Qajar dynasty were consistently silent toward *taʿzieh* and tolerated it; some

[7] The following saying from the sixth Shiite Imam Jafar Sadegh has played a significant role in establishing the importance of crying and mourning for the Karbala event: 'anyone who composes or cites poetry for Imam Hossein and then cries or makes one cry shall be forgiven by God and placed in Heaven'.

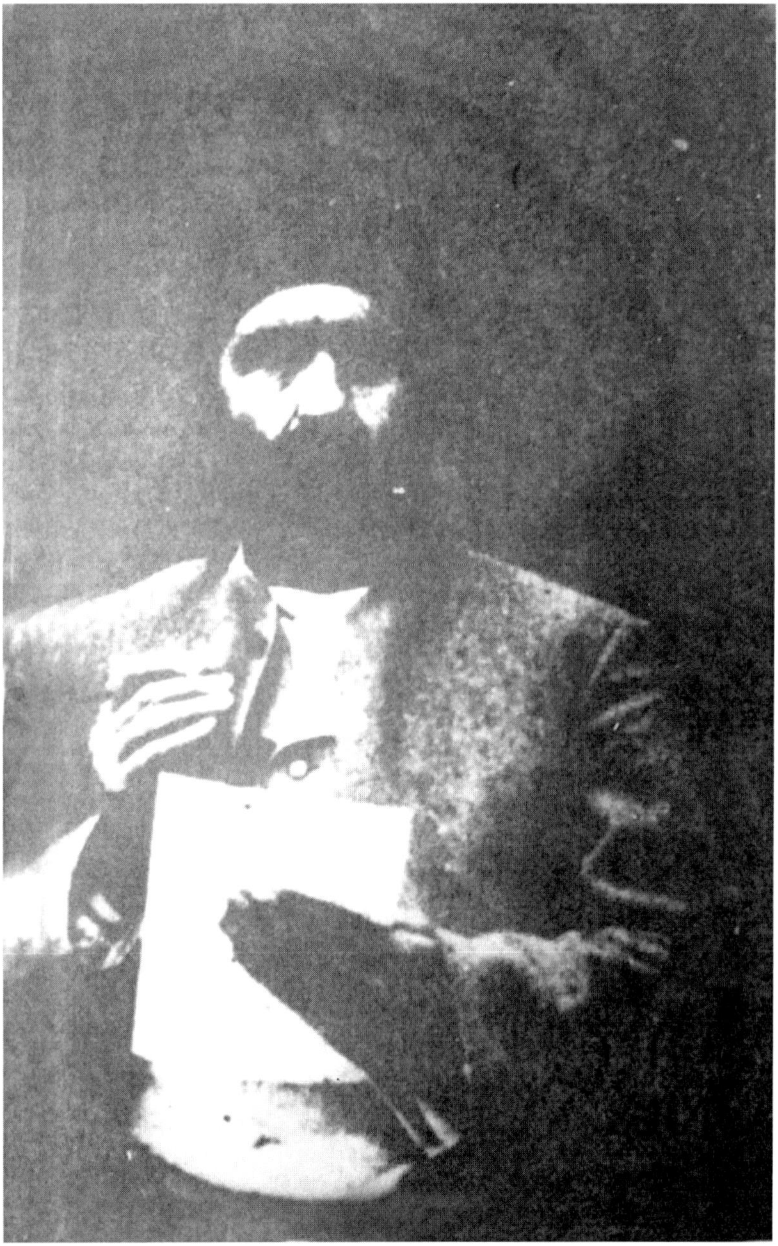

Figure 8: Mirza Aghayih Tabrizi, the first Persian screenwriter.

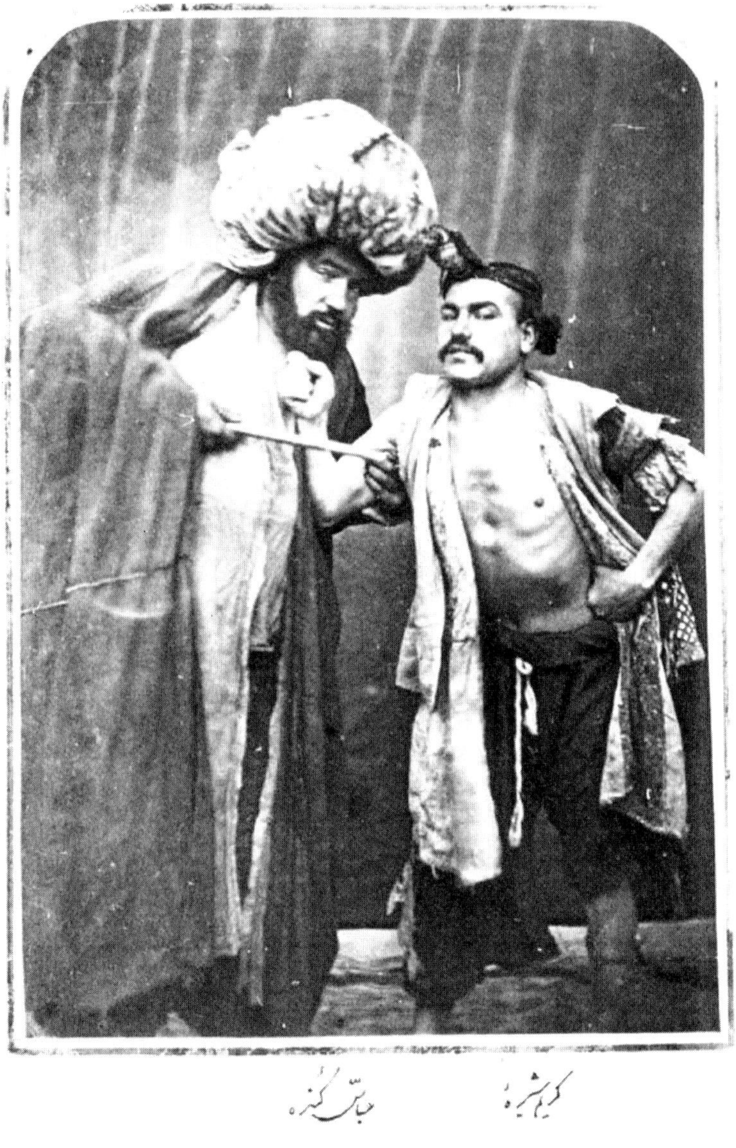

Figure 9: Karim the Junkie and Abbas the Big.

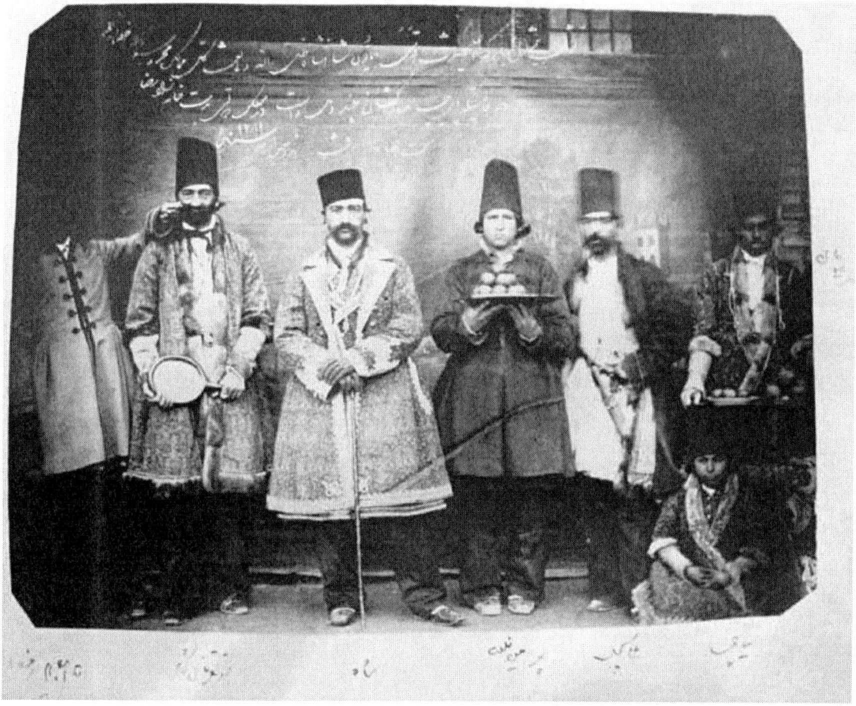

Figure 10: Nasser al-Din Shah alongside the muqalids in his court.

issued *fatwas* regarding its acceptability (Shahidi 2001, pp. 120–21). There were three problematic kinds of *tashabuh* for the clerics in *ta'zieh*: *tashabuh* to imams, *tashabuh* of women to men (as men played the roles of women in *ta'zieh*), and *tashabuh* to nonbelievers and the enemies of the sacred.

An analysis of the texts of the *fatwas* that were influential in the promotion of *ta'zieh* delineates the attention paid by the clerics to *ta'zieh* performers. While not holding any knowledge of theatre, they emphasized *tashabuh* and automatically distinguished the task of a *shabih-khan* from that of theatrical actors. The first *fatwa* that opened the way for *ta'zieh* during the Qajar era was issued by Mirza Abulqasim ibn Hassan Gilani (Mirzayih Qumi 1738–1815). Together with the clerics who followed him, he accepted that *shabih-khans* could wear women's costumes, as the one and only objective of *ta'zieh* was making people cry. This was against the backdrop that, according to clerics, men wearing women's clothing was a forbidden act and subject to severe punishment. Yet, among the photos of *muqalids* one finds many examples of men wearing women's garments merely to make people laugh (fig. 11). Hence, it is indisputably evident that the clerics tried to prevent the infiltration of the elements of *taqlid* and theatre within *ta'zieh*. In their approach, men wearing women's costumes was simply another manifestation of theatre, *taqlid*, and mere entertainment.

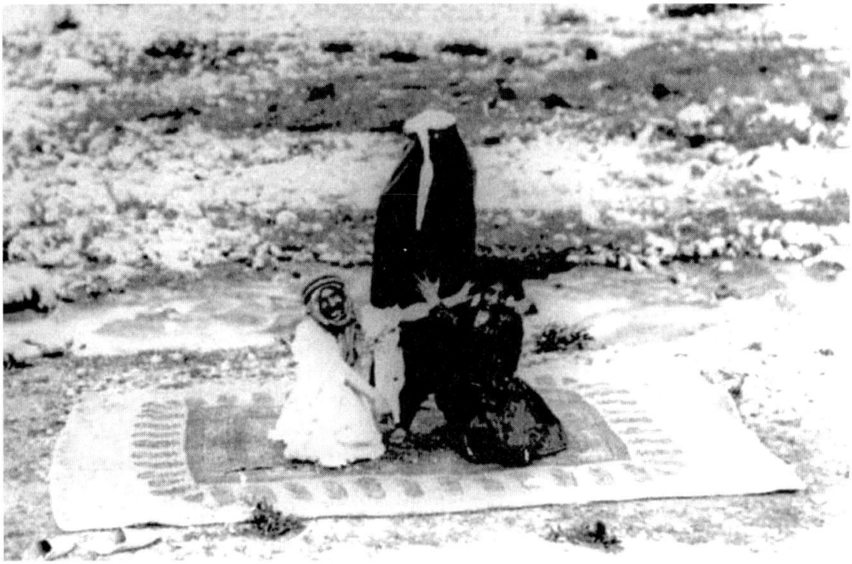

Figure 11: Two muqalids who had accompanied Nasser al-Din Shah in a royal summer residence.

Influenced by Mirzayih Qumi, many Islamic jurisprudents reckoned *shabih-khani* as a religiously acceptable act but stressed that *ta'zieh* should be solely *shabih*, or similar to the Karbala event and not itself. For example, Siyid 'Ali Yazdi (1941, p. 171) elaborated on Mirzayih Qumi's *fatwa*: that *ta'zieh* is not a case of *tashbih* of one person to another; rather, it aims at a case of *tashbih* of a condition, costume, and state of mind for crying. Another senior scholar, Alamih Aqa Muhammad 'Ali Kirmanshahi (2000, p. 329), writes that the purpose of *tashabuh* is to the imams by means of their goodness of character, authority and will, such that this *tashabuh* would engender sorrow, crying and mourning.[8]

These paradigms did not find their way to *taqlid*, however, and *taqlid* continued to remain as a threat to *ta'zieh*. Authority, gender, ethics and the private domain of people's lives were sources of making the audience laugh in *taqlid*. To this end, *ta'zieh* that made people cry through *tashabuh* and *taqlid* that made them laugh using hyperbole constituted the two contradicting poles of Iranian drama. Ironically, both held one commonality: the essential quality of both forms can be summarized in their seeking similarity of one to another. Another phenomenon in the Qajar period that bore this characteristic was, of course, photography.

The term *shabih* also had another application in the Qajar period. Prior to the extension of the Farsi word *'aks* for photo, daguerreotypes were also called *shabih*. Such verbal usage by people like Kamalolmolk (1846–1941) referring to one of Richard's daguerreotypes has been documented (Zoka 1997, p. 8). The use of the word *shabih* for daguerreotypes as well as for *ta'zieh* and narrative religious painting (fig. 12) clearly expresses the emphasis on the difference between the original and the copy in Qajar culture. Interestingly, both the *shabih* of the imams in *ta'zieh* and the *shabih* of the shahs and political dignitaries in photos were deemed invaluable and highly respectable. They were not counterfeit and worthless copies, but copies that contained the spirit of the glory of the original within them. This is perhaps why the photos of the Qajar era turned into instruments to display the power and the glory of the king.

Concluding remarks

Prior to representing an acting technique in Iranian theatre, the nontheatrical state of *shabih-khans* and the theatrical poses of *muqalids* are the first step for discussing the issue of *tashabuh* and representation in Iran's culture and art during the Qajar dynasty. There are three issues which reflect three different kinds of *tashabuh*: *ta'zieh*, which is a *tashabuh* to the sacred; *taqlid*, which is a hyperbolic *tashabuh* and, in effect, a kind of parody;

[8] For more information in this regard, see: Tabatabayi 1984; Shahidi 2001.

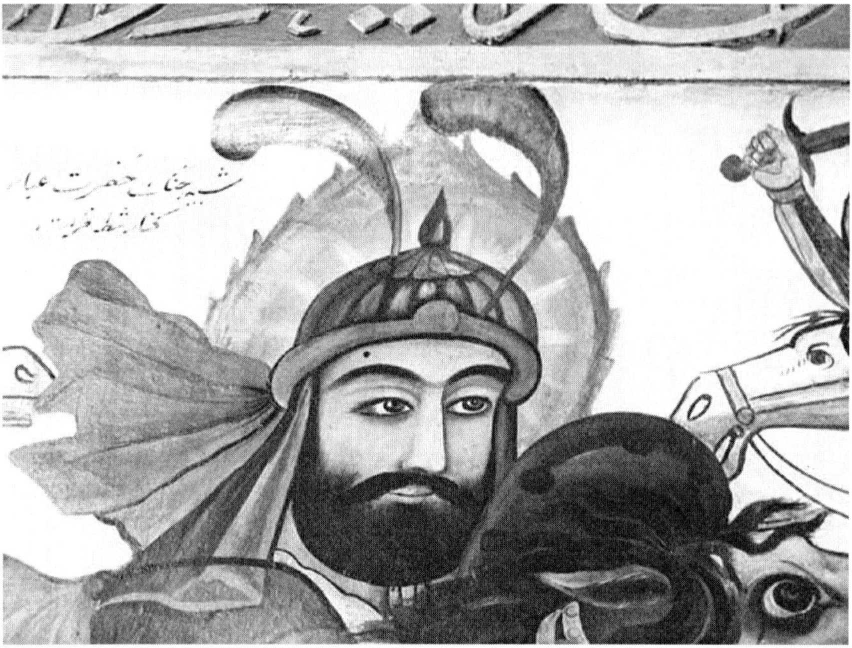

Figure 12: Mural painting of Imamzadeh Shah Zayd Isfahan.

and photography, which is a *tashabuh* to reality and contains the greatest degree of similarity to its original. Further analysis of these three phenomena elucidates why the similarity of one thing to another during the Qajar era was problematic for the clerics and aroused antagonistic reactions. The discussions of Mulla Hadi Sabzivari, who considered photography philosophically impossible,[9] are another vivid example of the controversies of the clerics over *tashabuh*.

The Qajar era was indeed a unique period with contradictions: we find controversy surrounding the issue of *tashabuh* on one side and the shahs' advocacy and promotion of cameras on the other. People would watch *taʿzieh* in a hall commissioned by Nasser al-Din Shah, which was very

[9] Mulla Hadi Sabzivari was a senior cleric of the Qajar era, who, before seeing the camera or learning what it was, stated that the reflection (or, in his words, 'shadow') of the form of a human on a sheet of paper or glass plate without the owner of the shadow is philosophically impossible (Zoka 1997, pp. 48–53).

similar to Western theatre halls, while *taqlids* in the king's court and on the streets among the common people were also important. This was to the extent that the scenes of *taqlid* performances were recorded with any instrument possible, be it films or shots.

As a result, the inattention of Nasser al-Din Shah and Mozafar al-Din Shah to *tashabuh* bore a profound impact on Iranian art in several aspects. The early introduction of photography, the development of a specific kind of narrative painting, the promotion of *ta'zieh* and the introduction of cinematography in Iran were products of the recreational approach adopted by the two Qajar kings with the obstacles of any kind of *tashabuh*.

The disfigured and the abnormal captured by the lens of Qajar era photographers

Alireza Nabipoor

Introduction

Creating objects is of high importance in photography. The photographer inadvertently changes people into objects by making them things to be seen (Solomon-Godeau 1991). Following the advent of photography and its early introduction into Iran, as well as the warm reception that it received from the kings, almost everyone in the imperial courts took to this new art form (Adle 2001). A number of photographers used the technique to record certain subjects that either had not been possible for painters to record or simply did not appeal to earlier artists.

Several photographers who were in contact with the Qajar court depicted scenery, buildings, and the like in addition to photographing the king and his imperial court. Considering Nasser al-Din Shah's interest in photography, a number of photographers travelled with him or other court dignitaries in order to photograph different buildings and tribes (Zoka 1997). Amidst all this, some of the interesting subjects for the photographers of the time were those individuals who seemed abnormal in some way or another.

This study reviews the attitude of photographers as a sector of society in the Qajar period toward these abnormal and disfigured individuals and the ways in which this attitude was represented in their photography. More than 10,000 photos from the Qajar period are available in the University of Tehran Central Library and Documents Centre; the author gained access, however, only to a number of the photos of the disfigured and abnormal and studied them within the following five categories:[1]

1. the physically disfigured,
2. those with nanism or dwarfism who had an abnormal appearance but were accepted by society,
3. the mentally disadvantaged,
4. *mughalids*, or Qajar era clowns,
5. the elderly whose senility had turned them abnormal.

The disfigured were mainstreamed in society but did not receive any special assistance or attention. In this paper, the relationship between the photographer and the subject is taken into consideration.

The physically disfigured

By definition, this group comprises those whose appearance is abnormal in some way and who, due to their deficiencies, are deprived from leading a normal life and in some cases are incapable of meeting their own daily needs. Their appearance catches other people's eyes.

In their frequent travels, the photographers of the Qajar period chose a number of these people as the subjects of their photography. Facing these people, the photographers did their best to show the deficiencies of their body parts. Therefore, the photos reveal that their producers were by no means demonstrators of the mental status or the social roles of the subjects; rather, the photographer used the camera only to document these individuals as interesting objects. In a number of available such photos, the attempt of the photographer to emphasize the subjects' deficiencies is perceivable.

Using simple backgrounds and decontextualizing the person from his/her everyday environment accentuates the portrayal of the deficiency fig. 1). Additionally, the inscriptions on the margins of the photos mention only the deficiency of the subject; the photographer provides no information about the cause of the deficiency and the ways that person faced the abnormality.

1 The author wishes to acknowledge the Script Division of the University of Tehran Central Library and Documents Center for their assistance in allowing access to the pho-

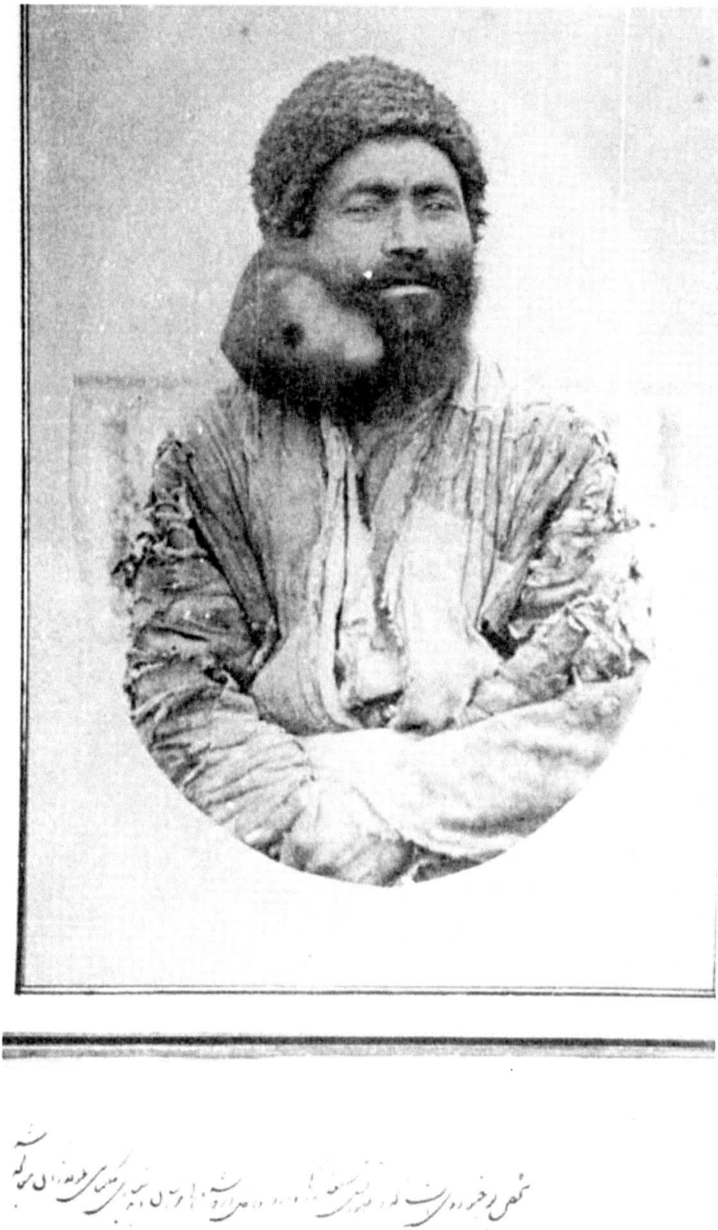

Figure 1: A man from Bujnord with a tumor on his head.

Facing the handicapped individuals, a number of photographers made them naked in order to attract more attention to the defected part, such that, sometimes, the person is actually marginalized by the abnormal structure of the body. (fig. 2)

The available photos of the disfigured from the Qajar period include a number of pictures of a man from Khurasan whose extensively deformed left leg was shown by a photographer from different angles. In these photos, by choosing the most striking perspective and putting the subject against a simple background, as well making his deformed part of body naked, the photographer turned the disfigured man into an object to be seen. In fact, it can be argued that the identity of this man lies in his defected leg; the deficiency of his limb is the reason he became the subject of the photo. This fact causes the photos to appear as images taken for the process of diagnosis, in which all of the aspects of a person's deformity are made deliberately visible. However, being aware of his deficiencies, the deformed man accepted being depicted as an object by the photographer (fig. 3–4).

The inscriptions on the photos can demonstrate the photographer's attitude toward this disfigured man, emphasizing the poverty and abnormality of the subject; no writing, of course, could portray as much as the photo itself does.

Sometimes in addition to the deformity of the disfigured individual, the overall manner was interesting for the photographer. In the inscriptions written on two photos taken by Agha Reza (1843–1889), the photographer of Nasser al-Din Shah's court (Zoka 1997), he first mentions that the subject had no hands and only after that did he note that the subject could write with his feet. The nakedness of the deformed subject and the inscription added by the photographer emphasize the person's abnormality. The photo provides no information about the lifestyle of the subject; only his ability to write with his feet, an extraordinary act, is mentioned (fig. 5).

A number of the disfigured subjects photographed during the Qajar period were children. Abdollah Mirza Qajar (1850–1909) – one of the most active photographers of this period, who took photos of many cities in Iran and accompanied Mozafar al-Din Shah Qajar in two of his travels to West-

tographs used in this study.

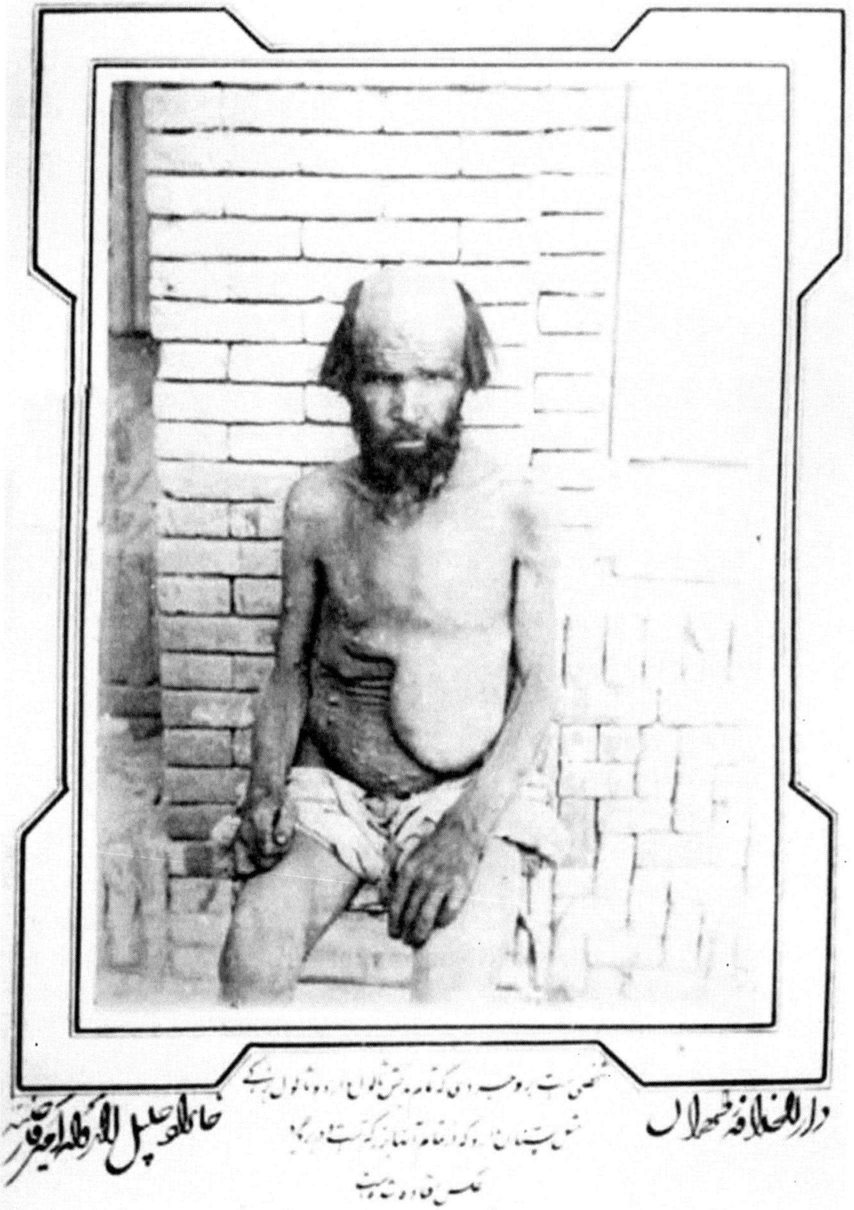

Figure 2: A man from Bujnord.

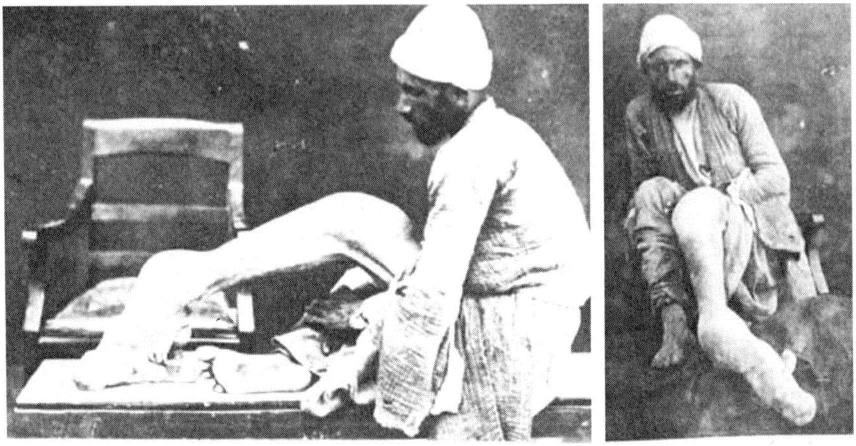

Figure 3–4: The man with the deformed leg from Khurasan

ern countries – took a photo of a six-month-old baby with physical defects. What catches the eye at first glance is the father, who posed before the camera contentedly despite his disfigured baby. This man has accepted his deformed child. The photographer, on the other hand, described the child in his inscription as being unsightly, without a tongue and with an abnormal head (fig. 6).

There were also disfigured females, with their number probably being equal to that of males; due to some cultural considerations, however, taking photos of deformed women was perhaps taboo. Generally speaking, the religious and cultural prohibitions of the Qajar era prevented photographers from taking photos of women, especially of their faces. Therefore, female subjects depicted by photographers often were the photographers' relatives or poor people who were paid for posing as subjects (Etehadieh 1994; Sheikh 2008). Among the photos made available to the author, only one had the subject of a woman with a certain deformity to her feminity (fig. 7). The inscription in the margin describes some of the costumes and cultural traditions of Iran during the Qajar period.

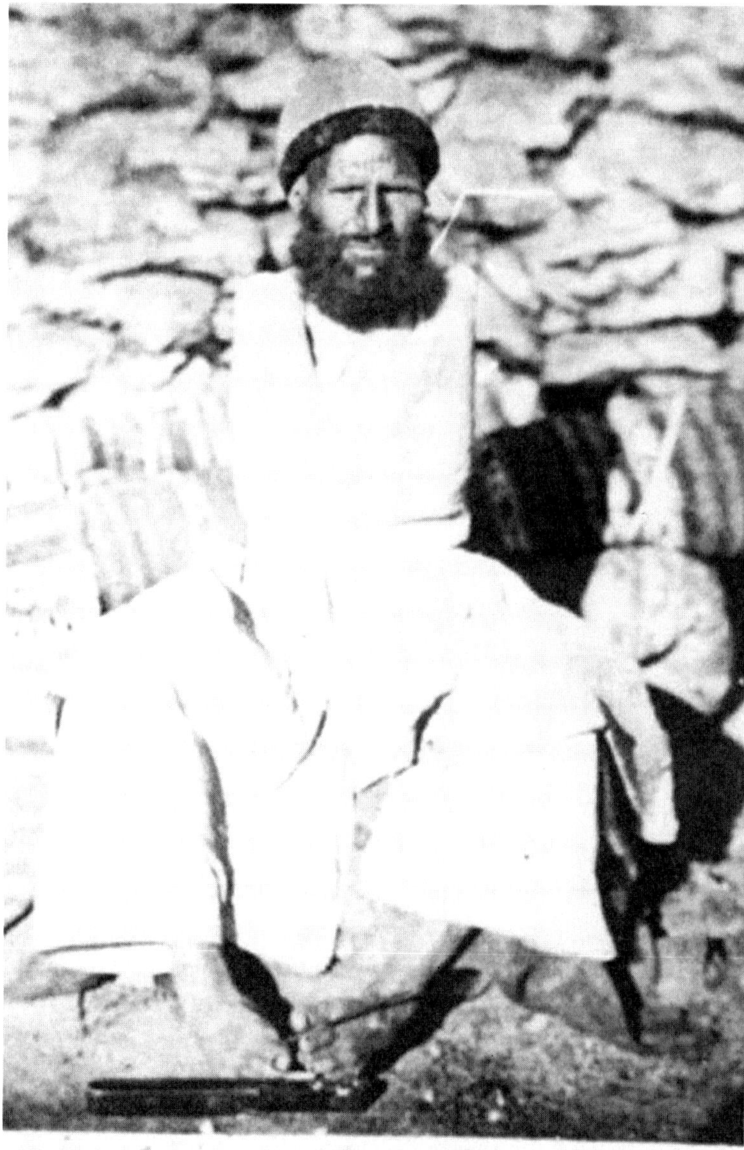

Figure 5

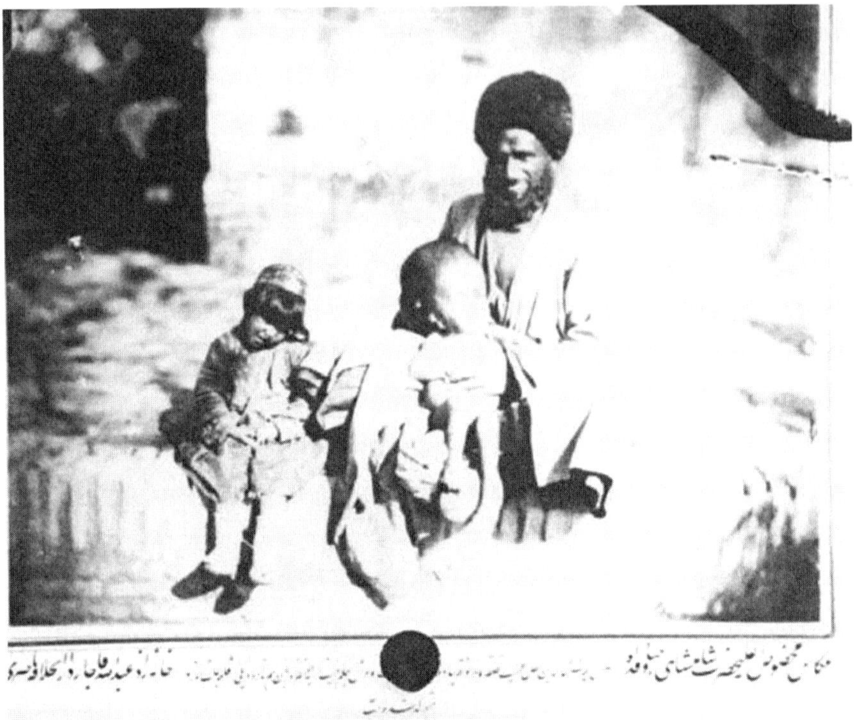

Figure 6

Those with Nanism or Dwarfism

Dwarfs may be classified within the category of disfigured individuals. They share many characteristics as well as a more typical lifestyle and social position; thus, the photos of this group of people are studied in an exclusive category.

Despite the defect in their anatomy, in the photos of the Qajar period, dwarfs are seen performing different social roles. Generally, Qajar photographers adopted a more neutral attitude toward this category of individuals in comparison to the other types of disfigured people.

For instance, in family photos of dwarfs, the popular arrangement of typical family photos of that time was observed: the father is seated at centre with his sons around him. Furthermore, by using a common back-

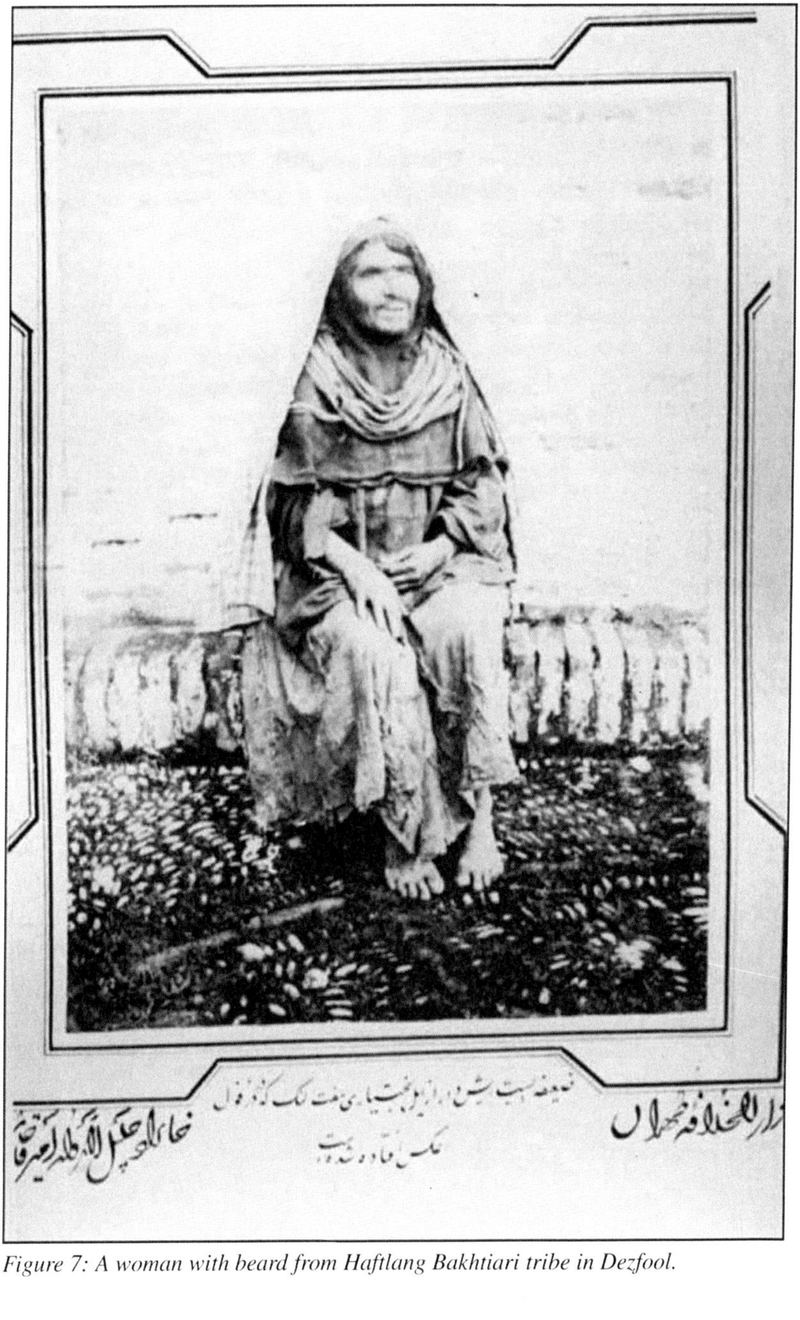

Figure 7: A woman with beard from Haftlang Bakhtiari tribe in Dezfool.

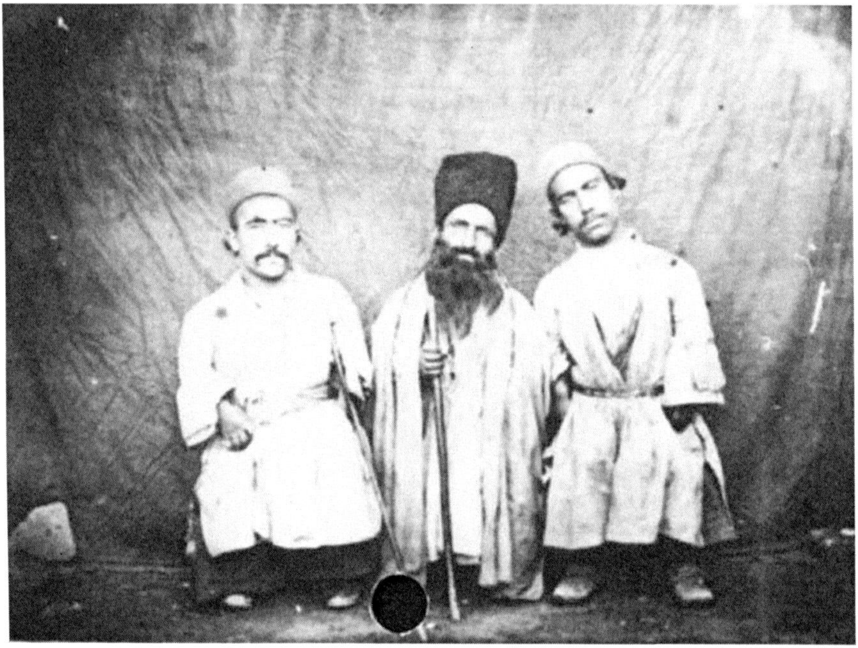

Figure 8

ground and choosing an appropriate angle and arrangement, the photographer deemphasized their defect in the photo (fig. 8)

Among photos of dwarfs are two images of a dwarf cleric pictured next to a chair, which was used as part of the décor in photos from the Qajar period. The direct and stern look of the cleric, his social position as a mullah and the proper height of the camera all deemphasize his abnormality (fig. 9).

This attitude of photographers toward dwarfs is traced even among commonly short people. In (fig. 10), the very short man photographed is from one of the villages in Iranian Azerbaijan.

The Mentally Disadvantaged

In addition to those with body defects, there is a group of individuals whose mental and behavioural abnormalities separate them from the society in

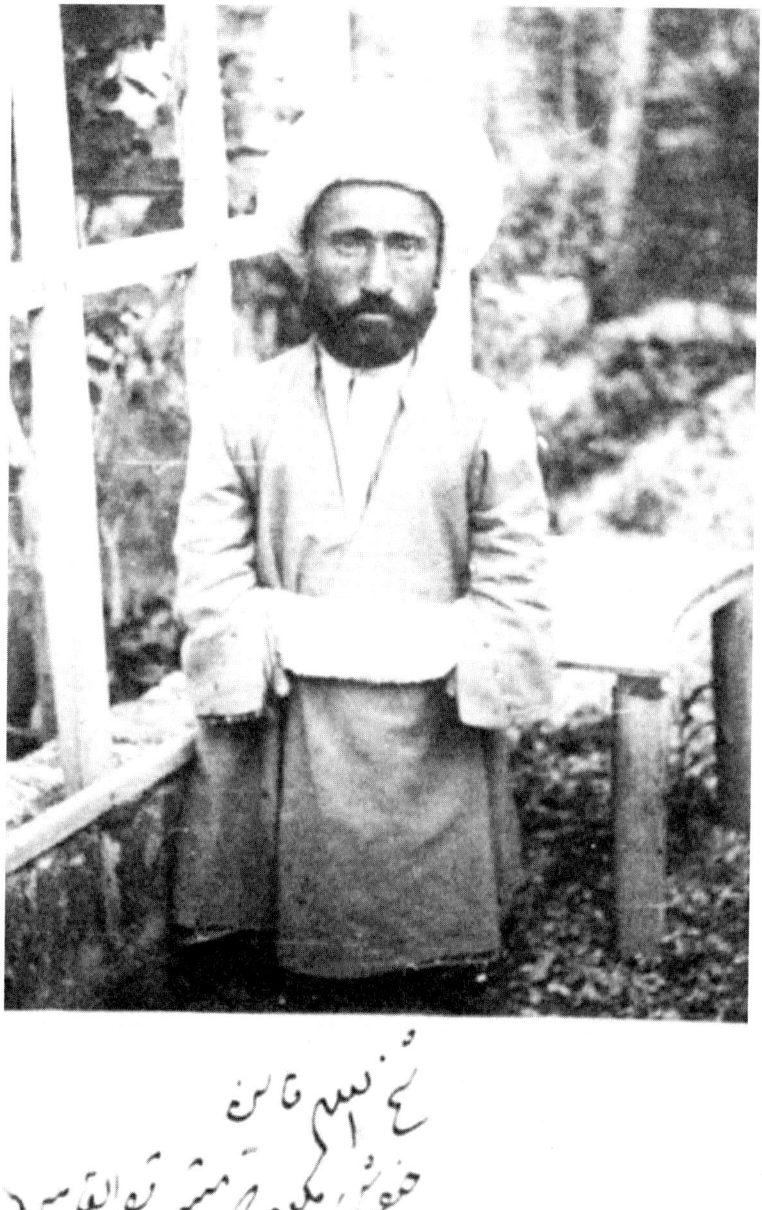

Figure 9

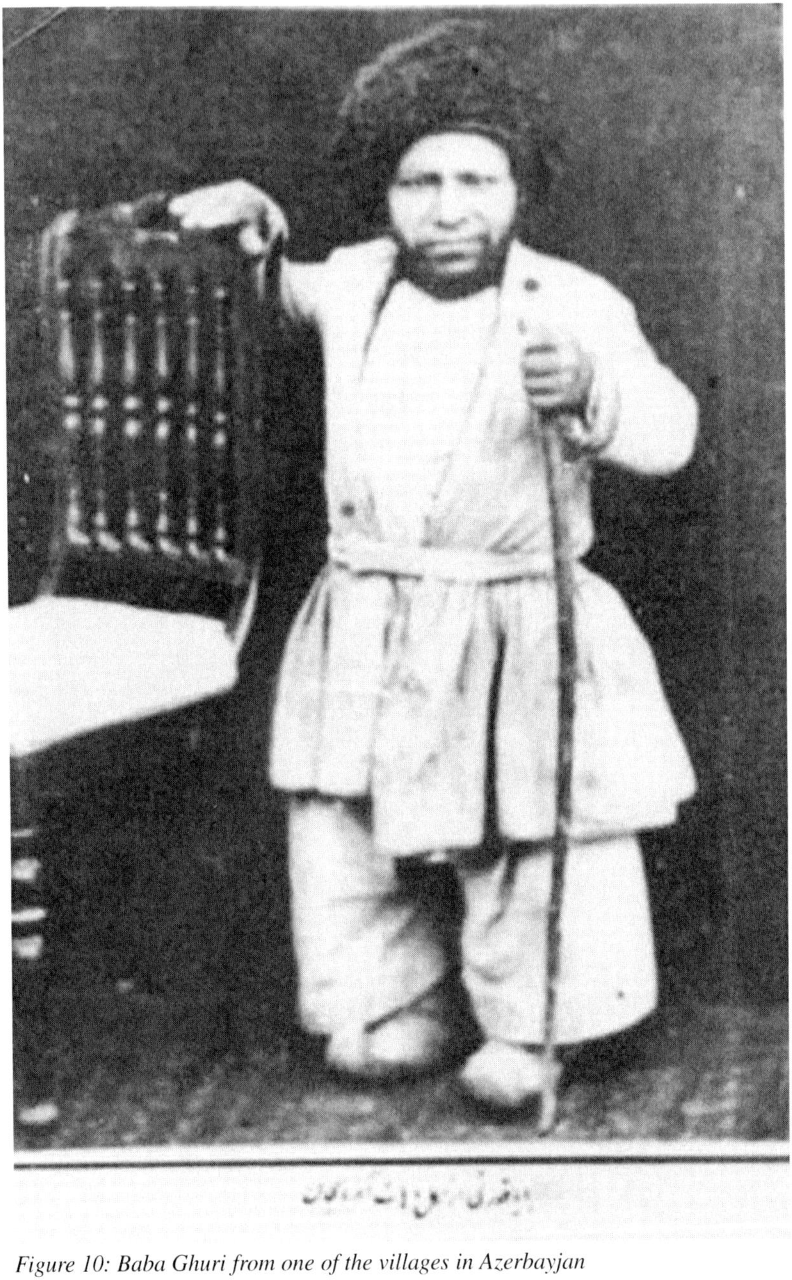

Figure 10: Baba Ghuri from one of the villages in Azerbayjan

which they live. The most important aspect that makes these people different from other deformed individuals is their lack of a correct understanding of the daily affairs of their life.

The photographers of the Qajar period were of course interested in picturing the mentally disadvantaged. Being fully aware of the limited cognition of his subject, the photographer would turn the mentally disadvantaged into an object to be portrayed without the subject's knowledge that he was being used as a tool in the photographer's hand.

In some cases, the photographers pretended that their cameras were guns and chased and threatened the subjects. The fear of facing the camera is clearly visible in the faces of these subjects (fig. 11).

The fundamental point in photos of the mentally disadvantaged is these subjects' unawareness of their inclusion in the photos (figs.12–13). The dominant – and to some extent impolite – attitude of the photographers while taking photos of the mentally disadvantaged in that era is completely visible. In some cases, the photographer violated not only the social rights of such individuals but also their basic human rights.

Mughalids and Clowns

In every society there are people who are marginalized from the mainstream due to their specific vocational and social stances. Although they have no physical or mental deformities or abnormalities, members of this group turn into a somewhat abnormal or deviant social walk of life because of the aforementioned stance.

During the Qajar period *mughalids*, or clowns, were among those classes of people who led a separate and secluded life from the rest of society due to the specificities of their job. Although they were welcome on stage to perform hilarious acts, which included foul language and sexual jokes, they were not at all a respected social class off the stage. It was this very different stance that they held that encouraged Qajar photographers to take photos of them.

Reviewing the photos of *mughalids* reveals a number of differences between the ways they were represented and the manner in which aforementioned vulnerable individuals were depicted. As a part of their occupation,

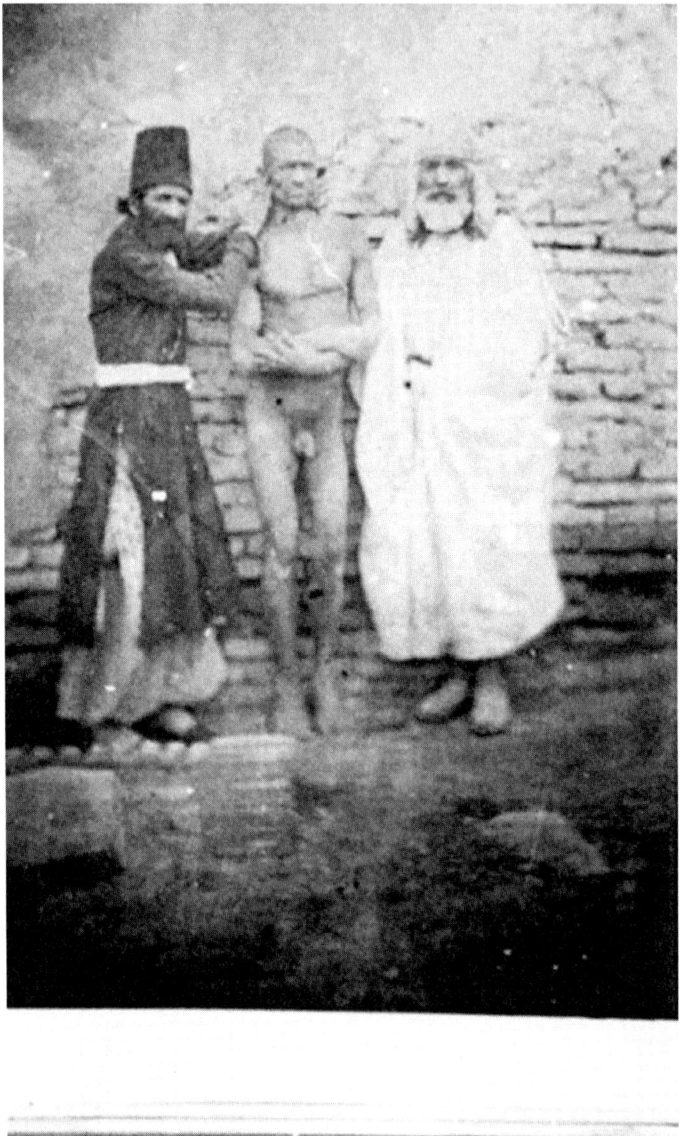

Figure 11: Dervish from Ghuchan, an insane person.

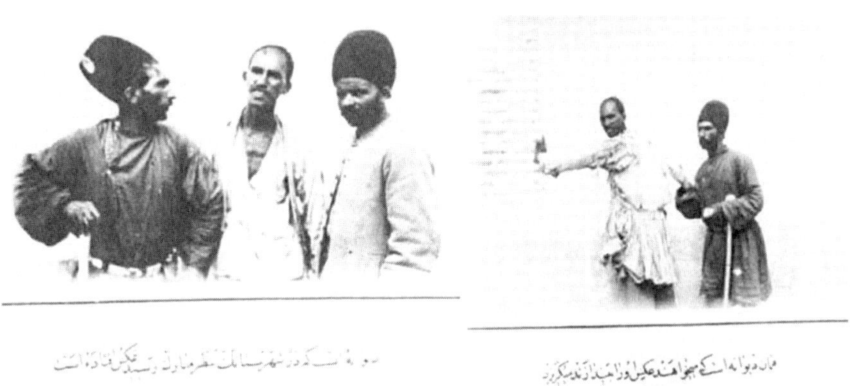

Figure 12–13: An insane person in Shahristanak.

mughalids were used to being the subject of photography. Therefore, they were very confident in facing the camera. The photographer resorted to showing only the facts of their jobs and their outlandish appearance; contrary to the depiction of the aforementioned vulnerable people, photographers simply marvelled at picturing these subjects (fig. 14).

Wearing worn-out clothes and masks and adopting abnormal gestures and poses in front of camera are demonstrative of the *mughalids'* full awareness of being subjects and desire to be seen. Hence, it can be argued that in these photos the subjects are superior to the photographers, which might explain why the photographers could not note much about the subjects in the margins of the photos (fig. 15).

The elderly people

A part of every society is composed of the elderly. Among this group are those whose body structures have become deformed due to their senility. Such physical features made them appealing to some photographers, who selected them as subjects for photography.

The available photos from this period and their inscriptions make two aspects of old age visible: first, the age which is clearly delineated in the bodies and appearances of these people. With their worn-out clothing and humped backs, these old people pose in front of the camera. The second aspect that gave these old people an air of abnormality is the photographers'

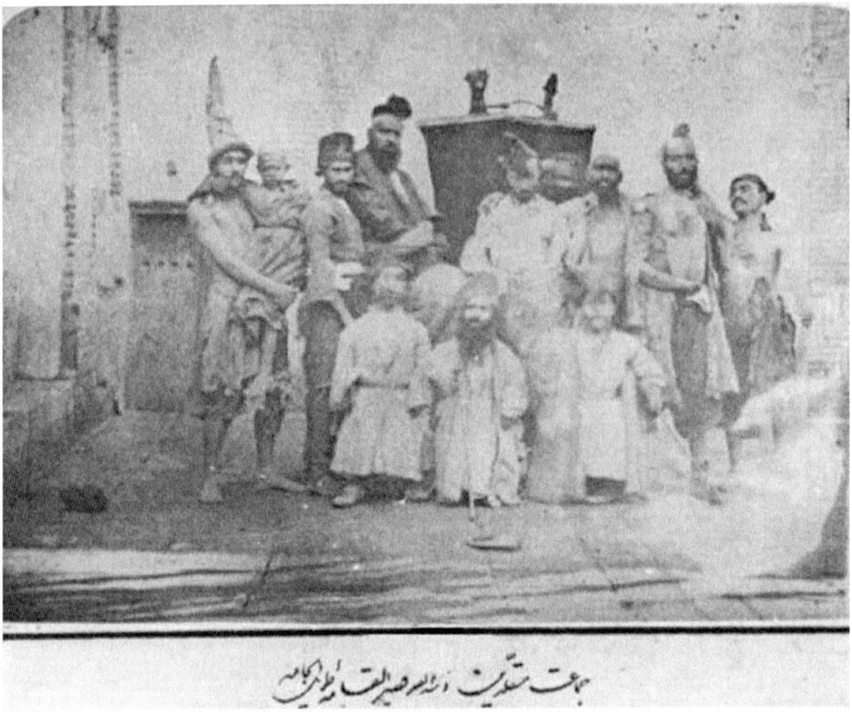

Figure 14: A number of mughalids and three dwarfs with long clothes

inscriptions and angles. By putting these people in the centres of the images, photographing from a front angle and providing notes in the margins, the photographers remind us of the photos of convicts in penitentiaries. In the inscriptions the photographers emphasized the exact age of the subjects and, accordingly, elucidated them as abnormal members of society (fig. 16).

Concluding remarks

This chapter investigated the ways in which photographers captured different groups of disfigured and abnormal individuals during the Qajar era by studying the available photos as illustration documents that express the vision and the interaction between the photographer and the subjects who are different from mainstream society.

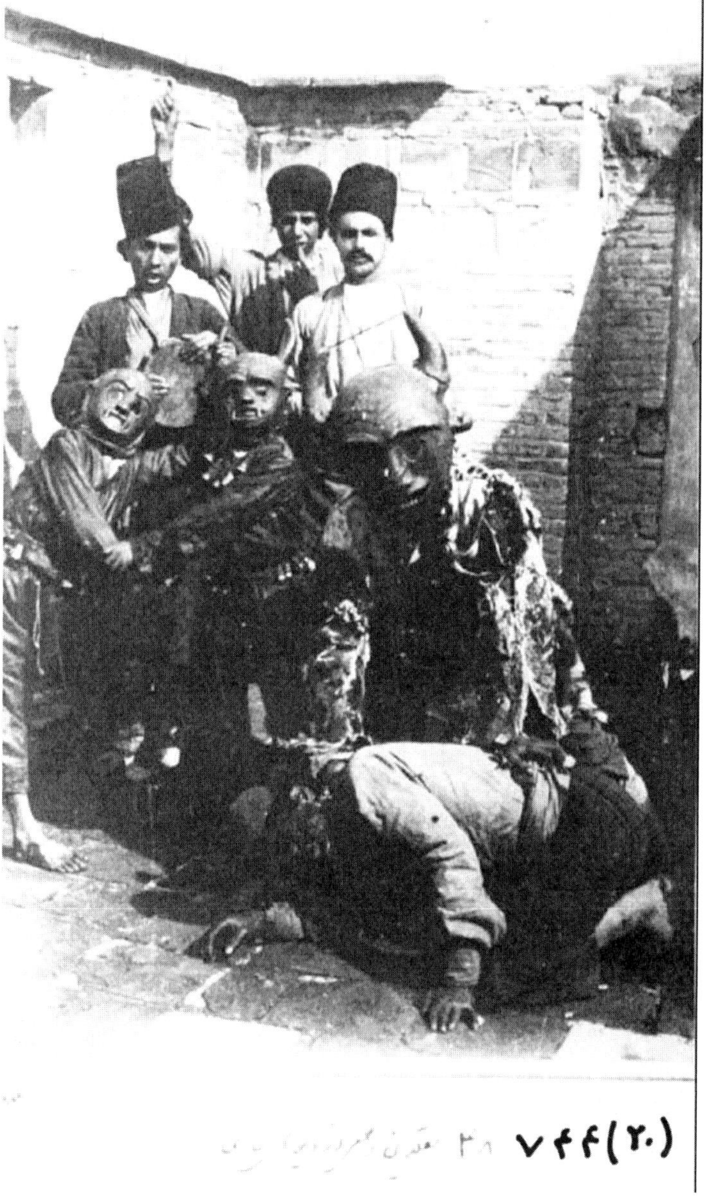

Figure 15: Mughalids and a number of actors dressed as Div, Sari.

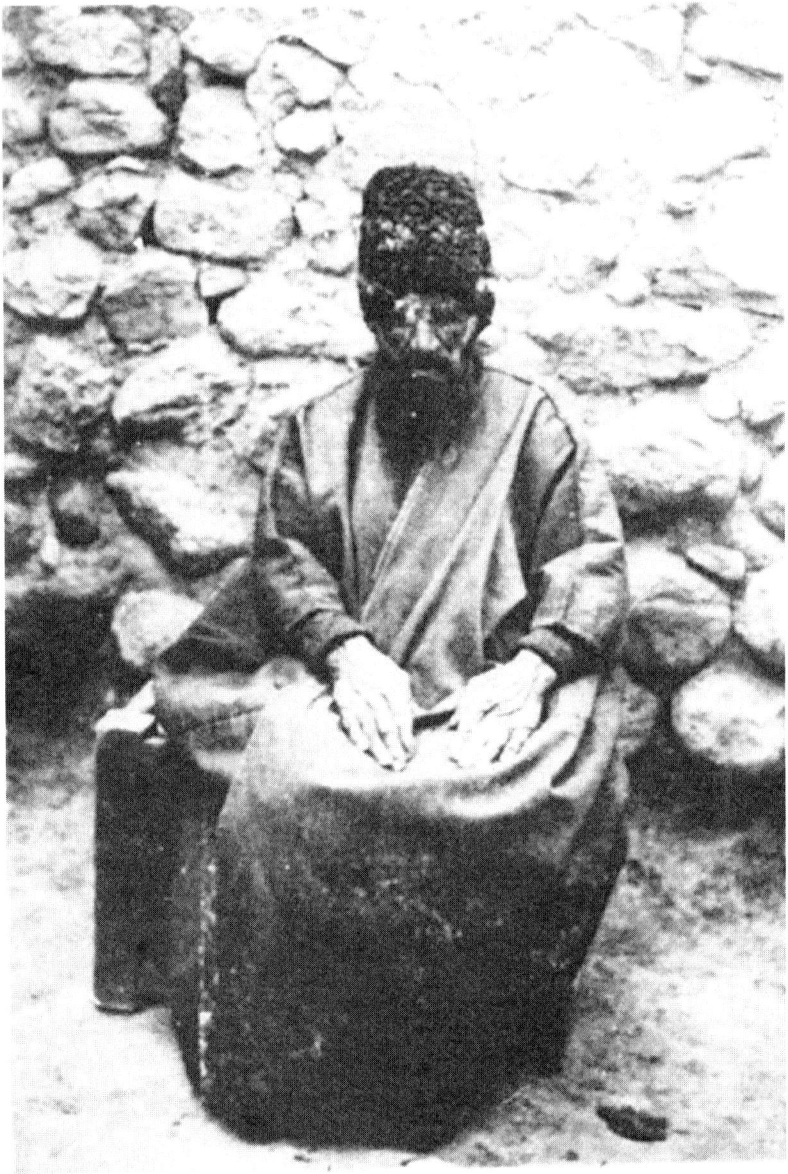

Figure 16

Photography was of course affiliated with the imperial court upon its introduction into Iran, and photographers thus were selected by courtiers. Consequently, most subjects of photography lost their self-confidence due to two issues: first, the equipment they stood in front of with no understanding of its structure and mechanism and, second, the photographer himself as a person who held a higher position than they did. It is amidst this cognizance of their weakness that the subjects were preparing themselves for the shoot.

The aspect of the photos which perhaps attracts the most attention is the inscriptions. The significance of these writings is based on the fact that the subjects did not interfere with them and it was solely the photographer who provided his comment and judgment about the subjects, with his own personal and unilateral vision.

Photography and recognizing historical changes of the Qajar era: a new historical view

Ali Mohammad Tarafdari

Introduction

Historical photos have always been interesting and can be studied from different perspectives. During the Qajar era– and concurrent with the emergence of the art and industry of photography in Iran – cameras captured many cases and moments concerning the lives of the people and politicians as well as various events and incidents according to individual, family, political and religious considerations. Because the photos are considered objective documents, sometimes they can be used by historians and researchers of social history for the review and recognition of existing historical data and findings. The role the historical photos can play from this viewpoint is at times unique. They are objective and documentary examples of historical data, which can range from few to numerous in volume. Moreover, historians may not be able to differentiate correct data from different and sometimes contradictory examples; thus, historical photos and films can play a major role in proving or rejecting a historical judgment or interpretation. From this point of view, a historiographical consideration of historical photos is differentiated from other artistic and technical approaches: a historian considers historical photos from a particular view and, by using them as reliable historical documents, tries to deepen his/her historical studies, reviewing and critiquing the available historical data vis-à-vis the related photos.

Qajar era photos and review of Iran's social situation and historical developments

1. Geographical origin of some Iranian ethnic groups

In general, migrations inside Iran during the Qajar era – when it was easier for people and tribes to move according to demographic, political and economic considerations in view of Iran's vastness and the lack of today's political borders – can be considered one of the most important debates regarding Iranian social history. Of course, migrations have occurred during all periods of Iranian history and, naturally, different peoples' internal migrations during the Qajar era throughout Iran also occurred due to state obligations and for political and economic reasons.

However, due to the registration of the images of people from different Iranian ethnic groups through photography or film, the grounds have been provided for conducting different studies by relying on such objective documents. Particularly, cultural and racial links across Iran have emerged between the country's indigenous tribes and the migrants from the borders of the country as a result of internal immigration, some of which continues to the present day. Thus, a leading documentary aspect of the photos remaining from the Qajar era is that they have provided the evidence required to compare and evaluate issues such as the appearance and clothing of various ethnic groups, changes to their attire, racial and tribal specifications and the extent of change to or continuity in these features and characteristics during recent centuries.

Moreover, these kinds of documents can determine the geographical origin of Iranian ethnic groups in the lands around contemporary Iran. A documentary, classic and academic collection of such photos has been published in the book *Contribution to the Anthropology of Iran*, authored by the American anthropologist Henry Field. It may be the most unique work of research concerning the anthropological studies of various ethnic and religious groups in Iran. Of course, the photos in this book have been registered and recorded on the basis of anthropological studies. However, the collection can be studied as a set of unique and innovative documents. The following two photos from the book depict the Jews of Isfahan and the black people of southern Iran. They also represent the social living conditions of these groups, the link of the African and Arab peoples with the residents of the Iranian coasts of the Persian Gulf, and the bidirectional migrations of the inhabitants of the Asian and African continents:

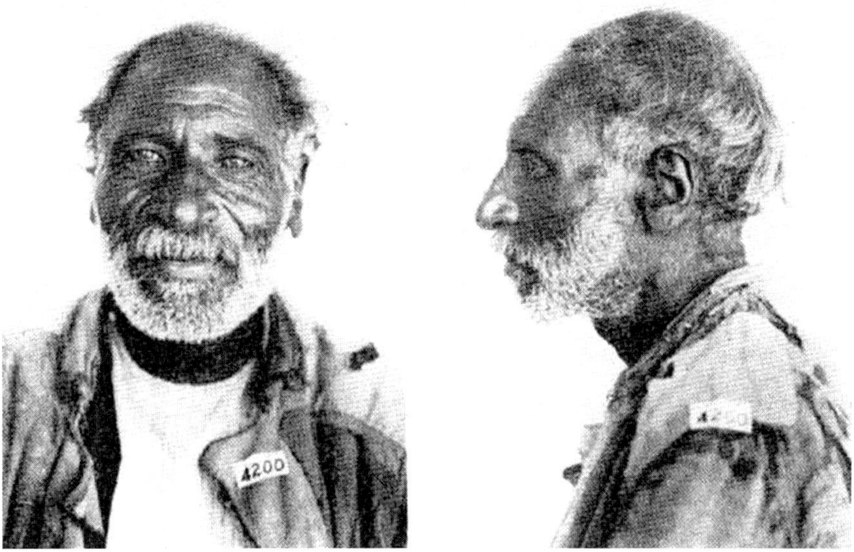

Figure 1: Jews of Isfahan (Field 1964, image no. 3497)

An important consideration regarding the photos taken in the Qajar court is the presence of young slave boys and girls in the court. Given the shortage of information in the existing historiographical sources regarding the social situation of these groups of court slaves, as well as the circumstances surrounding their exploitation, the debates concerning the slave boys and girls in Iran and other Eastern courts can be studied from a new point of view. This is especially true at a time when Western researchers, in reviewing the circumstances of the slave boys and girls in the Eastern world, generally have been influenced by the mentalities of the slavery of more recent centuries in the Western world and consider the mere presence of black slaves in Iranian courts an adequate reason for applying the generalized concept of Western slavery to black slaves in the East and Iran.

There are, however, fundamental differences between using slave boys and girls in Iran and the Eastern world and the slavery in the West during

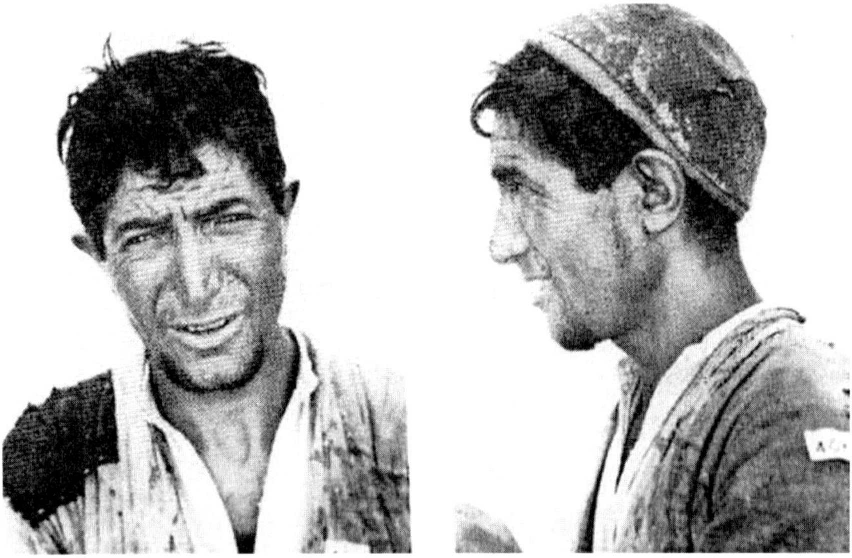

Figure 2: Black people (Field 1964, image no. 3368)

recent centuries. In this regard, the Qajar era photos can serve as objective documents relating the social status of the slave boys and girls in the Qajar court. However, the African immigrants living in southern Iran also were used as slaves to some extent. The photos taken from that period, such as the following example, confirm this theory.

2. Developments of and hierarchy in the Iranian army

In addition to the abovementioned issues, other important points, such as the ranks and hierarchy in the army and the weapons of that period, can be studied on the basis of the photos remaining from military forces. This approach would rise in significance especially at a time when the existing information in this regard is relatively sparse and there is little information in the historiographical sources of the Qajar era about the changes and developments that resulted from the modernization of the army; this situation restricts researchers to obtaining such information sporadically – and primarily through the military documents of the period. Therefore, the photos of the military forces of that period – especially those depicting uniforms

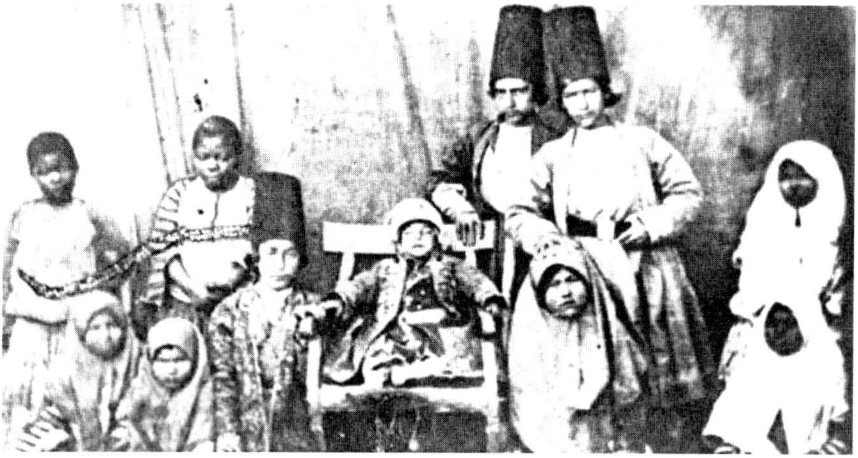

Figure 3: Mozafar al-Din Shah in childhood along with slave boys and girls, c. 1272 AH (Zoka 1997, p. 27)

and military ranks as well as the conventional weapons of that period – are of great importance in terms of studying changes related to the Iranian army system from the middle Qajar era to the First Pahlavi period (1925–1941). The following photo shows an example of the mentioned outfits and weapons.

3. Clothes of the court's women, statesmen and princes

The features and appearance of the clothing of the Qajar court's women, statesmen and princes is another issue that can be brought to light through the study of the photos of that period. Such photos can also complement the available historical data and even make possible the comparative analogy of the mentioned data. The clothes of the women of Nasser al-Din Shah's court (1848–1896) can be seen in the following photo; it is interesting to note that in this photo and others like it these women did not cover all of the parts of their bodies (i.e., their feet) while observing the *hijab* (the Islamic dress code) and covering their hair.

In the following photo the relative nudity of the upper body of one of Nasser al-Din Shah's wives is remarkable.

Additionally, toys are seen in some of the photos of the Qajar court's

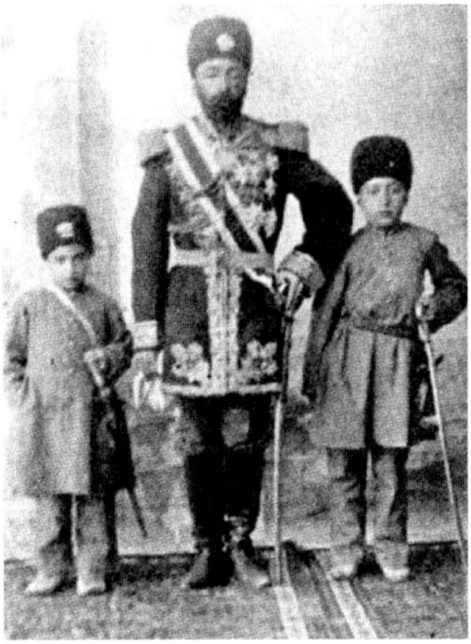

Figure 4: Malek Qassem Mirza with his sons, c. 1275 AH (Zoka 1997, p. 11)

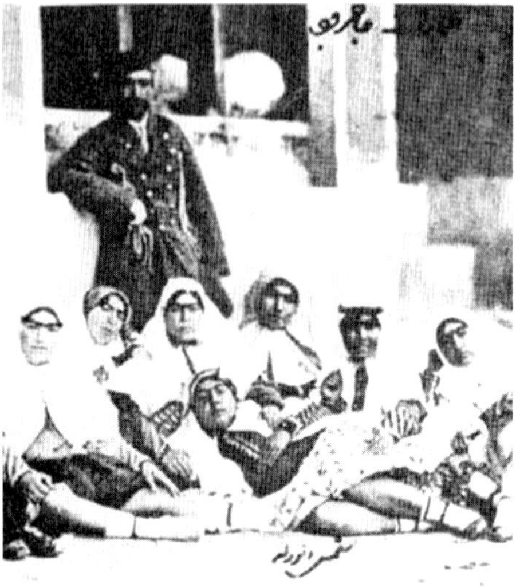

Figure 5: Nasser al-Din Shah and seven women of the harem, Jajerood, c. 1280s AH (Tahmasbpour 2002, p. 32)

children. Almost no information about children's toys exists in the historical sources of that period; hence, these photos can be used for studying the leisure of these young princes and children and even for rebuilding some of the obsolete toys used in that period. The following photo shows the kite of Kamran Mirza Qajar (1856–1927), which is different from today's kites.

4. Ceremonies of the Qajar era court, jobs of the period, the state of religious minorities and darvish groups and modernism in their clothes

The ceremonies and rituals in the Qajar court – and sometimes the nature of them and the way they were held – is a topic whose details may be found only in the memories of the statesmen and women of that court. At the same time, the photos taken of some of these ceremonies, along with the descriptions in the memory books, give us a more complete image of the details of various ceremonies and rituals in that period. Most available photos and written descriptions of Qajar era ceremonies concern the mourning rituals

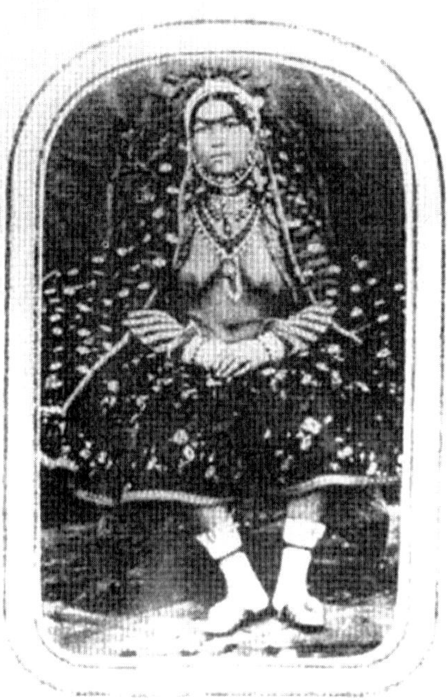

Figure 6: One of Nasser al-Din Shah's wives, c. 1290s AH (Tahmasbpour 2002, p. 32)

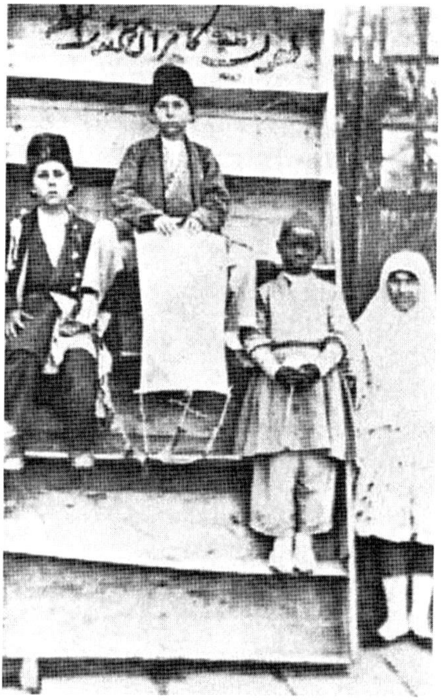

Figure 7: Kamran Mirza with a kite in his hand and one of his playmates, c. 1282 AH (Zoka 1997, p. 30)

of the month of Muharram, the rituals of *Tasuʿa* and *ʿAshura* (the day the third Shiite imam was martyred), *taʿzieh* (Iranian passion play) and other ceremonies, such as the contests of the holy Quran.

In the following image, six photos of the Quran contest as registered by Nasser al-Din Shah consisting of ceremonies for males and females are seen.

Common working conditions during the Qajar period are among other examples that have been recorded in the photos remaining from the period. One of these photos depicts the antique sellers in Tehran during the Nasseri period, which can be significant in view of the lack of any research concerning the procedure of dealing antiques during the Qajar period in Iran.

The significant point in the above image is the dealing in old books and

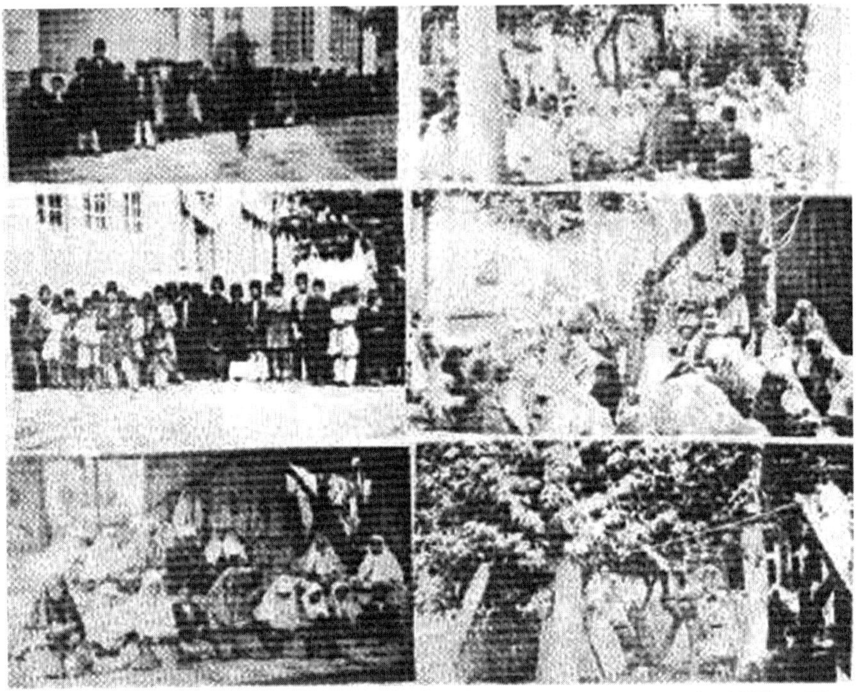

Figure 8: Six photos of a Quran contest in Niavaran Palace, 1295 AH (Zoka 1997, p. 33)

objects by a peddler, a practice that is still seen in Tehran's streets from time to time; it is probable that, as remains true today, the Europeans played a major role in the rise and spread of these kinds of dealings among Iranians.

There are also photos from the period – especially those taken by foreign photographers – that capture people of different ethnic and religious groups, like darvishes, as well as religious minorities. Such pictures make possible comparisons between the attire, tools and materials of historical itinerant religious groups and those of the people of current times. Moreover, the photos of religious minorities can show the probable amount of restrictions on the followers of other religions among Iranian Muslims. The following photos depict four examples of Iranian and Iraqi nomads, darvishes and Armenians.

Armenian women living in the Iraqi village of Challaveh: The shah

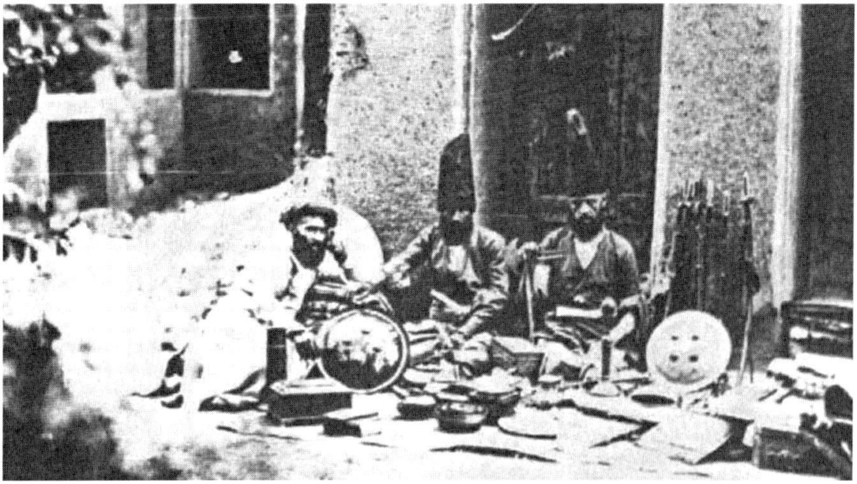

Figure 9: Antique market in Tehran, 1279 AH (Zoka 1997, p. 60)

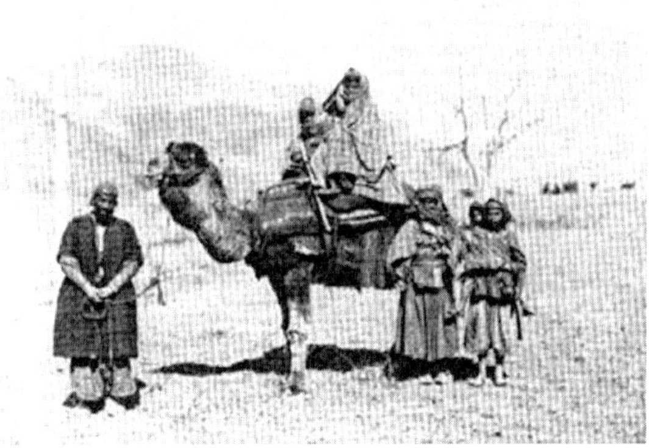

Figure 10: Hadavandi nomads, the Nasseri period (Tahmasbpour 2002, p. 68)

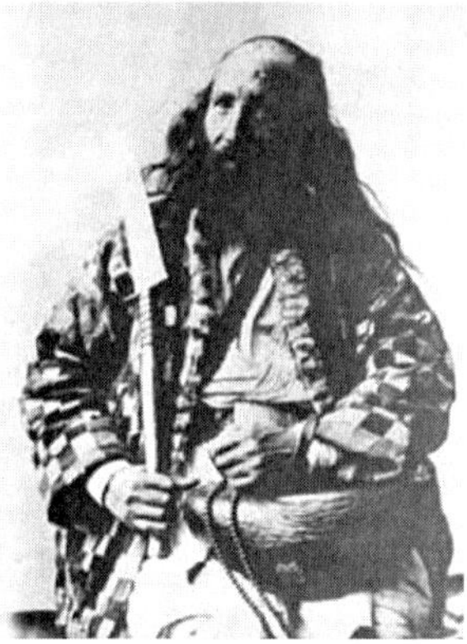

Figure 11: A Darvish with a drinking bowel and battle-axe, 1300 AH (Zoka 1997, p. 201)

had ordered the photographer to take the photo due to their clothing being strange in the Nasseri period (Visible Treasure 1998, p. 162)

Yet another significant point in the Qajar photos is the travel of Iranian statesmen and princes to Europe and the impact of such journeys on their tendency toward modernization, which is extensively reflected in the

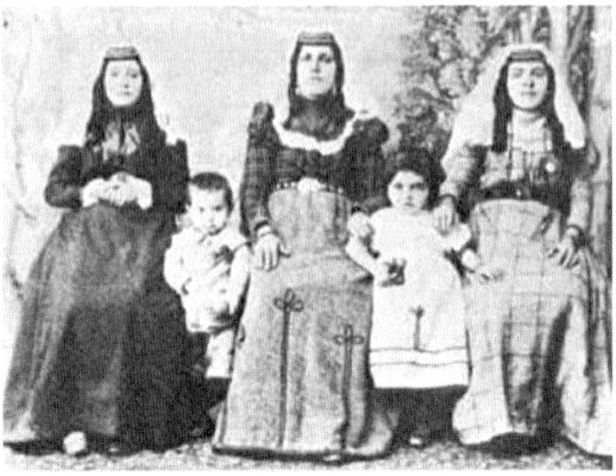

Figure 12: Three Armenian ladies wearing the special garment of Tabriz, c. 1330s AH (Zoka 1997, p. 206)

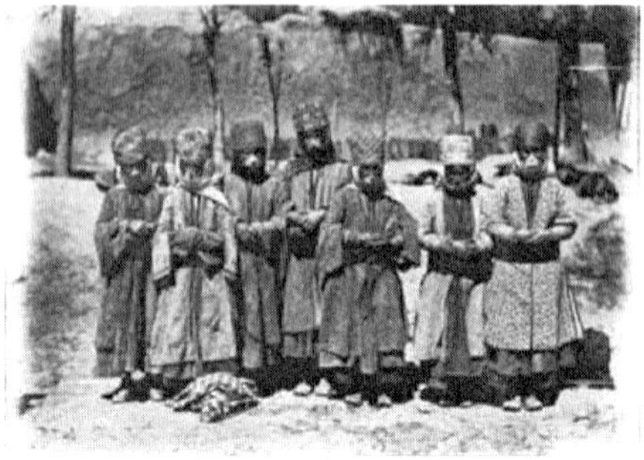

Figure 13

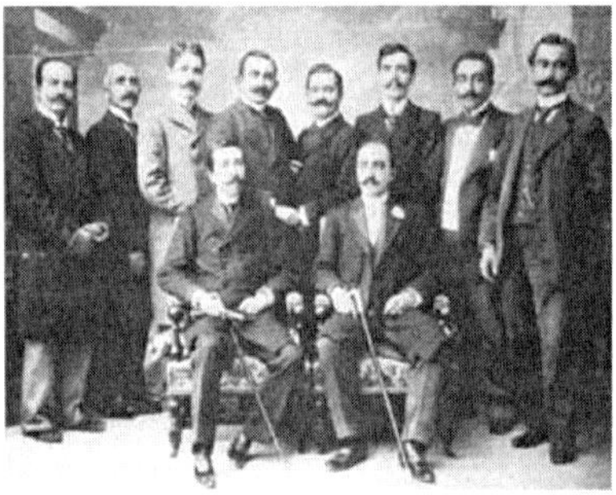

Figure 14: Mo'ayer-ol Mamalek, Mostowfi-ol Mamalek, Heshmat-ol Mamalek and several other Iranians, c. 1310s AH (Zoka 1997, p. 96)

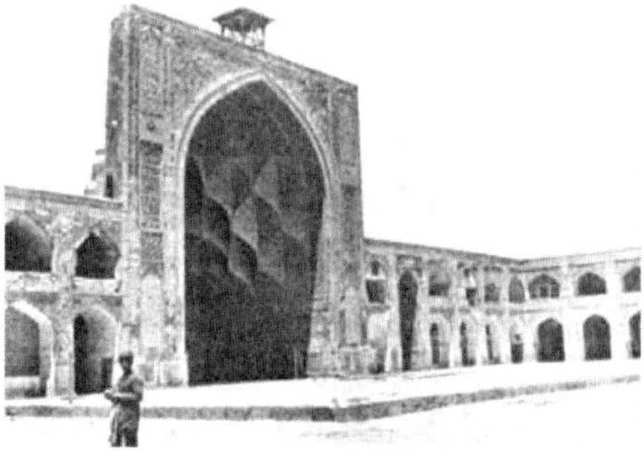

Figure 15: Jame' Mosque, Isfahan, late Qajar era (Zoka 1997, p. 177)

photography and historical resources of that period. One example is the following photo of a number of statesmen and aristocrats.

5. State of historical edifices and the structural changes in Qajar buildings

Perhaps the most important and illustrative point in the photos recorded during the Qajar era is that they have provided a pretext for reviewing and studying the changes and developments of historical edifices and the conditions of the buildings, places and towns of the Qajar era. These photos can amend much existing historical data and offer a more realistic idea

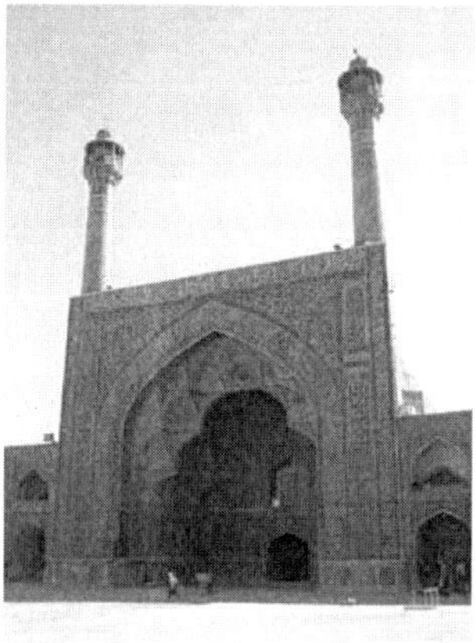

Figure 16: Jame' Mosque, Isfahan (source: the internet)

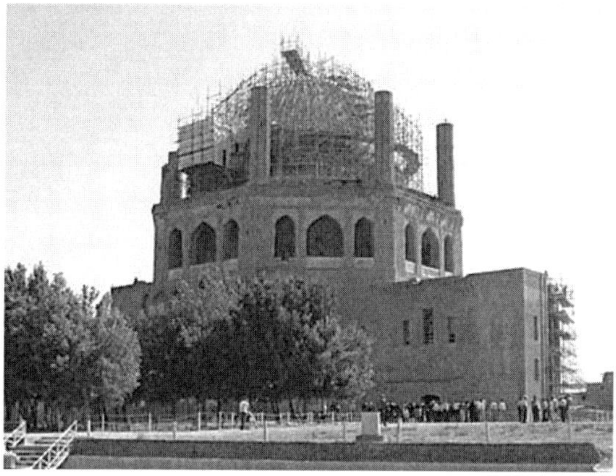

Figure 17: Soltanieh Dome, the Qajar era (Mokhlesi 1985, p. 60)

of the aforesaid structures to today's researchers. For instance, one of the most basic changes made to many Iranian religious sites was to the tile work of these buildings; comparison of the buildings' arabesque and the buildings themselves has often led researchers of architectural history to incorrect conclusions about the art and architecture of past periods. They can achieve better results by studying photos from the Qajar era, especially those related to repairs made to some of the buildings. For example, one can easily conclude that many of the existing tile works in religious buildings like mosques and mausoleums belong to older periods and were added during subsequent restorations.

The first photo from Isfahan's Jame' Mosque, one of the most important Jame' Mosques in Iran, was taken in the late Qajar era and early reign of Reza Shah Pahlavi. This photo clearly shows that the mosque had no tile work but brick decorations. Therefore, existing tile work belongs to the restoration done by Arthur Apham Pope (1881–1969) in the first Pahlavi era and subsequent decades. The repair and reconstruction have given a new face and façade to the building while erasing the original brick decorations. However, the decorations and changes added to the reconstruction that do not belong to the building's early period and original identity sometimes have been regarded as the typology of the tile works of the Safavid

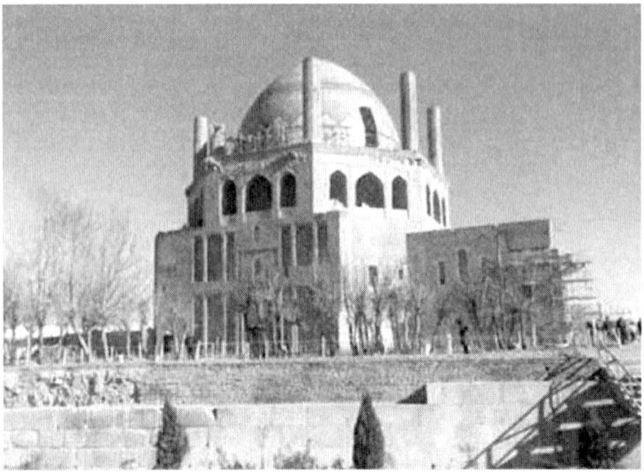

Figure 18: Recent image of Soltanieh Dome while tiling (source: the internet)

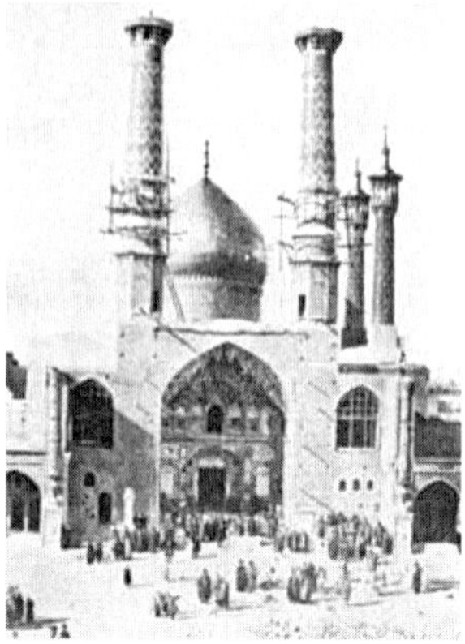

Figure 19: Recent image of Soltanieh Dome after the completion of tiling (source: the internet)

era (1501–1722) by researchers of Safavid history and Iranian architectural history.

Another noteworthy point is that the minarets on the two sides of the mosque's veranda are not seen in the first photo. Obviously, they are the corollary of the adjunctions and repairs of subsequent periods. Accordingly, the main identity of this edifice and the changes and restorations during subsequent periods can be unearthed by comparing early and current photos of the mosque. Furthermore, it should be noted that some of the recent tile works – especially following the 1979 Iranian Revolution – have featured Islamic beliefs to a large extent, and the names of the Shiite Imams have shone in the tile works of the façade of this mosque and others like it. The issue in some cases, like Soltanieh Dome, has completely changed the face and historical period of the edifices.

Lack of tile works in the early and original forms of religious buildings is seen in some of the most important such structures in Iran, including the Jame' mosques and the tombs of religious figures in different cities, demonstrating that these edifices have changed and developed to some extent under the influence of religious beliefs and the growth of the tiling industry in subsequent periods. Thus, researchers of architectural history as well as of

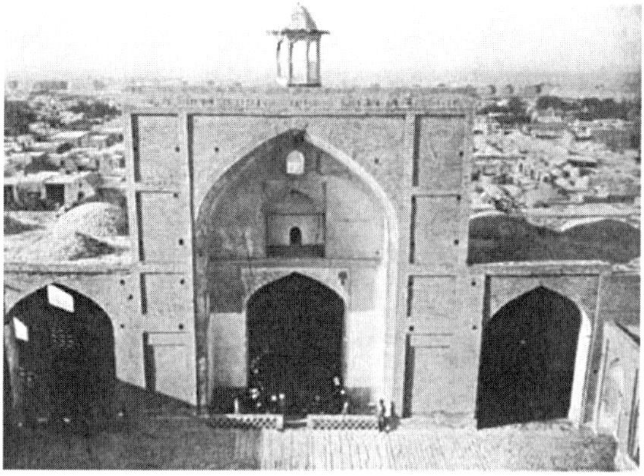

Figure 20: The veranda, minarets and dome of the holy shrine of Hazrat-i Mʿasoumeh, 1290 AH (Zoka 1997, image no. 70)

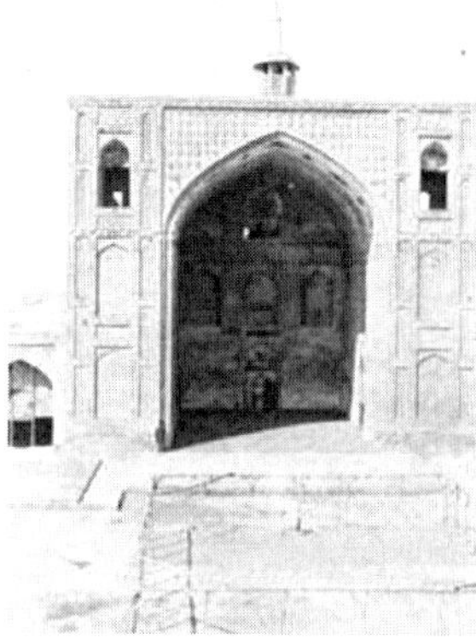

Figure 21: The veranda of Jameʿ Mosque in Sabzivar, c. 1290s AH (Zoka 1997, image no. 84)

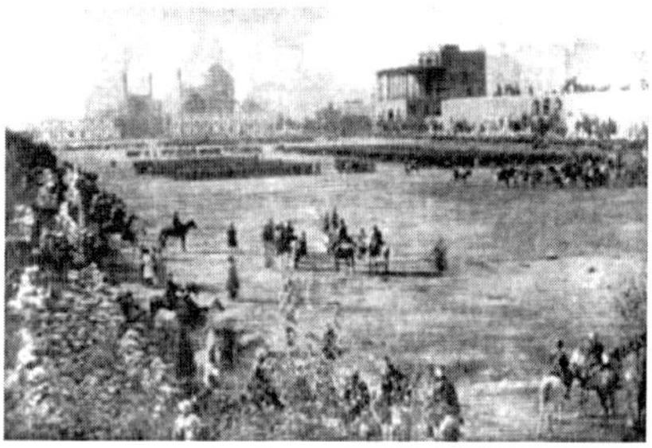

Figure 22: The veranda of Jameʿ Mosque in Neishabour, c. 1290s AH (Zoka 1997, image no. 85)

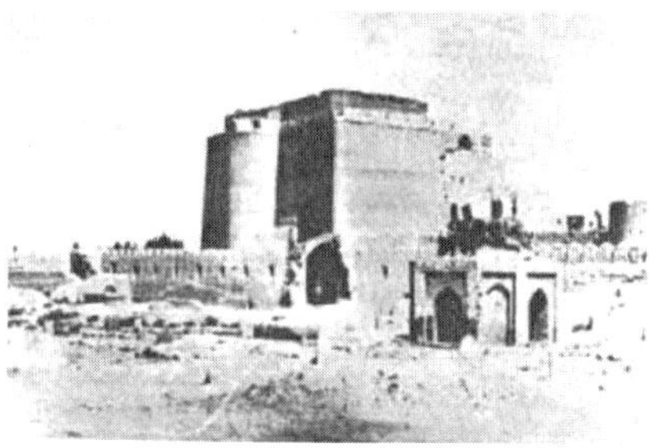

Figure 23: Military parade in Naqsh-i Jahan Square in Isfahan, the Nasseri period (Tahmasbpour 2002, p. 86)

social and political history must carefully refer to historical images of these structures in order to study the changes that sometimes led to entirely new buildings.

In the following examples, the original forms of the veranda, minarets and dome of the holy shrine of Hazrat-i Maʿsoumeh in the city of Qom; the veranda of Jameʿ Mosque in Sabzivar; and the veranda of Jameʿ Mosque in Neishabour are seen, clearly demonstrating that even the most significant edifices of Iran – that is, the tombs of Shiite Imams and dignitaries and the Jameʿ mosques – originally did not have many of their current ornaments.

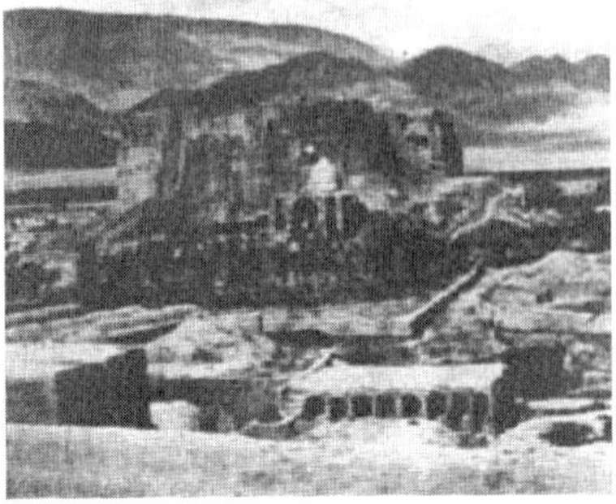

Figure 24: Tabriz Arg and Lellah Beig Cemetery, 1279 AH (Zoka 1997, p. 60)

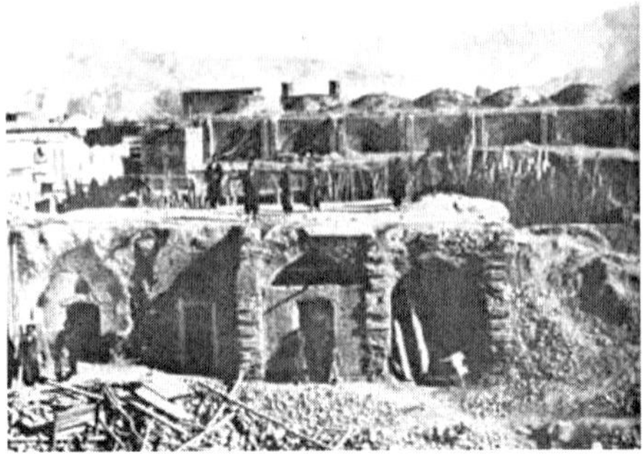

Figure 25: The view of Aradan village in Garmsar, 1313 AH (Zoka 1997, p. 106)

However, another significant point that can be demonstrated through the study of the registered photos of the Qajar era is the amount of change to the fabric and structure of Iranian historical cities and places during the recent one or two centuries. Thus, paying attention to this point can be more effective and crucial than studying the veracity of historiographical sources. For example, viewing the following image of the military parade in Naqsh-i Jahan Square in Isfahan during the Nasseri period, one can realize to some extent the vastness and main structure of the square during the period of Shah Abbas (1588–1629) as the main founder and builder of this square.

Additionally, the following photos show the state of Tabriz Arg (citadel) and the extent and shape of Aradan village and can be used as objective documents for studying Iranian architectural history and noticing the change of urban and rural fabrics in view of the destruction of Tabriz Arg during the first Pahlavi (for building Tabriz Park and the destruction of the city's garrisons), in the early 1980s, and in 1997 (for building the grand mosque of the city) as well as the destruction of the old fabric of Aradan village.

Finally, the following photo is, on one hand, a document confirming the historical data concerning the demolition of the Zandieh period (1750–1794) structures during Reza Shah and, on the other, among the only extant documents to portray the condition of some of these structures.

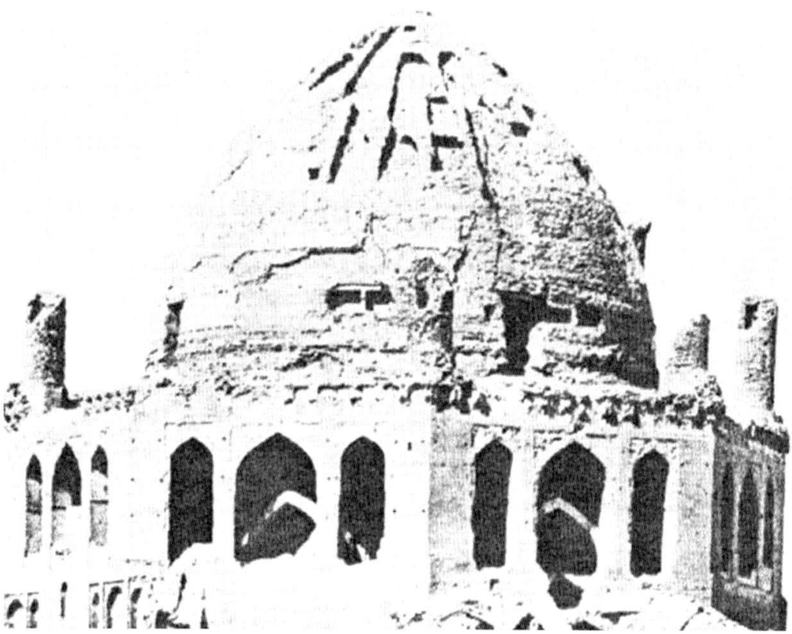

Figure 26: Destruction of the Karimkhani building (in Shiraz) during the construction of Pahlavi Street (Sane' 1991, p. 167)

Concluding remarks

In this brief study the author attempted to note the value and importance of photos as documentation of historiography and as a reliable and objective tool for measuring and studying the veracity of available historical data by presenting examples of photos from the Qajar era. There are, however, many other photos that could be referred to for the study of the points mentioned in this paper as well as illustration of additional points – the latter, of course, being outside the scope of this paper.

Comparative analysis of Iranian and foreign photographers' representations of the Qajar era

Abbas Amiri

Introduction

Applying a sociological approach to photography, this chapter seeks to explore the photographs of the Qajar era. Bearing in mind that the term 'sociology' was coined by Conte and that Louis-Jacques Mandé Daguerre invented photography in 1839 by publicizing his method for recording images on a metal plate, one might conclude that photography and sociology were born at the same time. For both, exploring and studying society was of great importance (Becker 1974).

Photographs are meant to be the outcome of photography. Viewing photographs, we can come to a kind of 'visual language', helping us understand the subject. This very process is of course done in sociology by using words. From the very first years after the invention of photography, images came into use by archaeologists, sociologists, orientalists and academics. The significance of photography lies in its ability to document and represent reality. In the nineteenth century it was common for photographers to travel to remote places such as Egypt, the Ottoman Empire and Jerusalem to produce photographic series. Sharing common borders with the Ottomans and Afghanistan (which was the gateway to India), the Iran of this period - the Qajar era- was cherished by Europeans. Thus, political representatives, who were often accompanied by professional photographers, found their way through Iran. These photographers were joined by their Iranian counterparts, named *ʿakkasbashi*, and as they began picturing Iran through their lenses the latter received practical training from the former.

The term 'photograph' in this chapter is operationally delimited to anthropological photographs, and foreign photographers are those residing in or visiting Iran but not originally born as Iranians, including Antoin Sevruguin (1830–1933). The historical period is of course the Qajar era.

History of Photography in Iran

Undoubtedly, the Qajar dynasty was highly influential in the early arrival of photography in Iran. Iran's geopolitical standing as well as its rich resources prompted Europeans to negotiate with the Qajars, especially Nasser al-Din Shah (Satari 2003); accordingly, foreign photographers visited Iran both to provide their own countries with photographic series of Iran and to satisfy the Qajar kings' longing for portraits. The first portrait, of Mohammad Shah (1808–1848), was taken by Nikoli Pavlov in mid-December 1842. Thus, photographic equipment made its way to Iran three years after having been invented. Following Mohammad Shah, Nasser al-Din Shah sat on the throne. Passionate about photography, the king ordered volunteers to be trained as *ʿakkasbashi*.

Based on their area of activity, foreign photographers were categorized into three groups: 1. photography instructors, such as Frances Carlhian (1818–1870),

2. photographers accompanying political and military representatives, such as Luigi Pesce (active 1848–61) and Luigi Montabone (?–1877), who visited Iran in 1864 and 1862,

3. freelance photographers who comprised two groups: the first included tourists such as M. Diolafao (1844–1920) and George Stevens (1880–1967) as well as archaeologists such as De Morgan (1857–1920), while the second group included photographers such as Sevriugin and Holster (1835–1911), who visited Iran in 1863 – this group made the largest contribution to documentary anthropological photographs

Anthropological Divisions

In order to make a comprehensive division of all of the photographers and photographs of the era, social grouping is applied. The first and the simplest

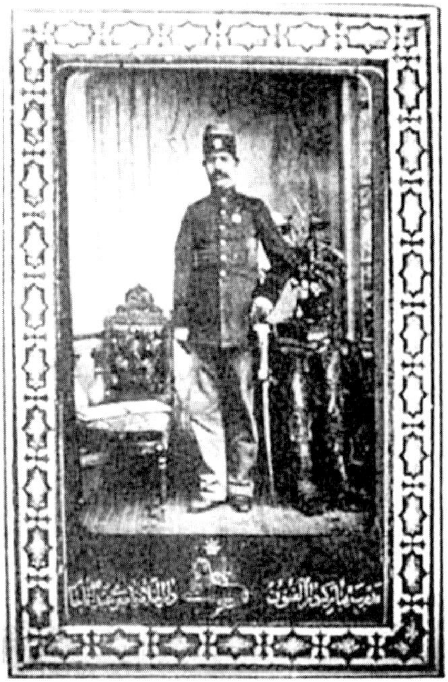

Figure 1: Mohammad Baghir Khan Sultan, Darolfonoon Photography Studio, Abdulah Qajar (photographer), University of Tehran Central Library.

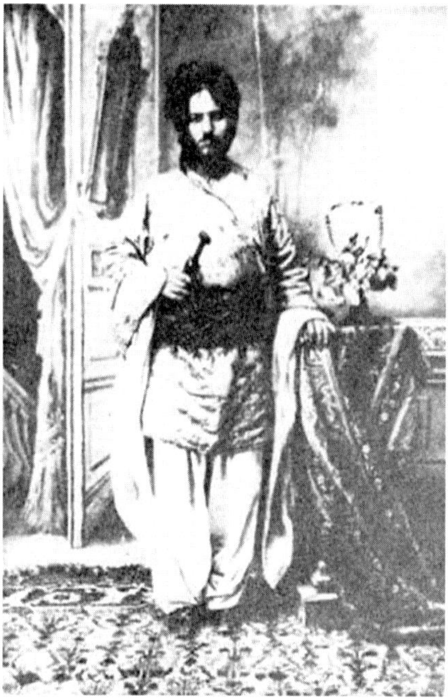

Figure 2: Kurdish man in local costume, anonymous photographer, University of Tehran Central Library.

means of categorization is according to gender. Indeed, photographers have demonstrated this very categorization in their images. The first Iranian photographs were taken of men, by men; most were portraits of the king and his men. In single or group portraits, Iranian photographers intended to capture the majesty, superiority and power inherited by men.

The settings were inspired by Western decorations. Sometimes Iranian photographers reproduced oriental images by Western photographers by juxtaposing Iranian men with Western settings and decor.

From its very first stages, documentary photography inclined toward images with models staged in or outside the studio. Thus, photography was entangled with reproducing the reality it encountered. Accordingly, such photographs were mediated to have a virtual and allegorical structure (Sheikh 1999).

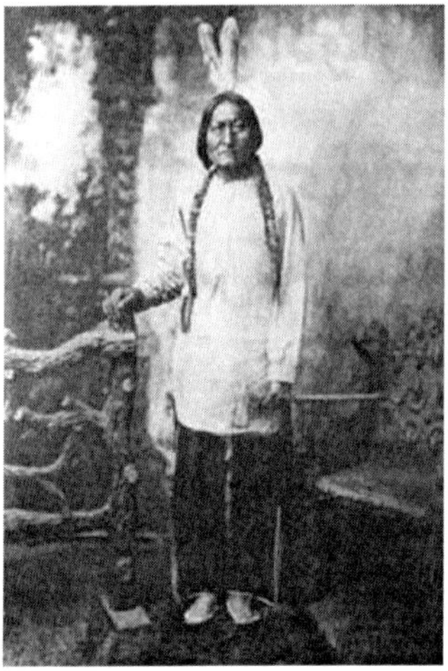

Figure 3: The 1870s, anonymous photographer.

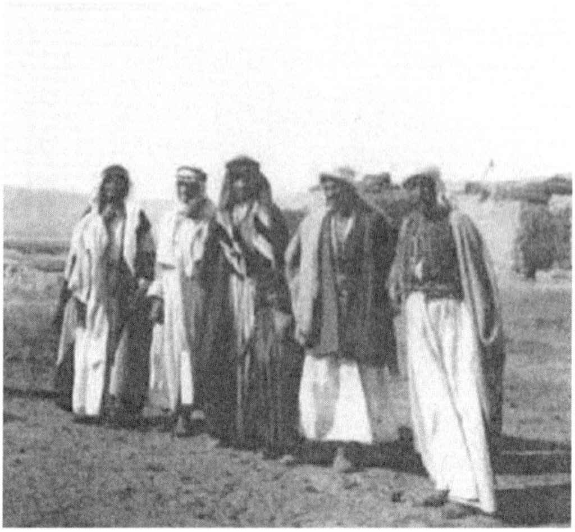

Figure 4: A group of men with Arab costumes outside a village, George Stevens (photographer).

When picturing men (with the exception of monarchs' portraits), foreign photographers primarily intended to depict their subjects in a palpable, down-to-earth way rather than focusing on power. These photographs are documentary visual commentaries of a specific group of Iranian men. Iranian icons, including carpets or textiles, were used by foreign photographers for the first time.

Occasionally, such technical issues as colour adjustment were employed to load the photograph with more information. For instance, Montabone created an image that was manually tinted and serves as a document of the colour of the uniforms of soldiers and servants as well as some of the architectural decorations of the palace (Tahmasbpour 2006).

Photographing women was not welcomed in Iran due to religious and traditional doctrines prohibiting male photographers from picturing women who were not their direct kin. The following three groups of photographs can be studied within this category.

Nasser al-Din Shah's permanent and temporary wives and the women of the Qajar royal family were probably the first Iranian women photographed. These simple photographs are in a sense considered to be family

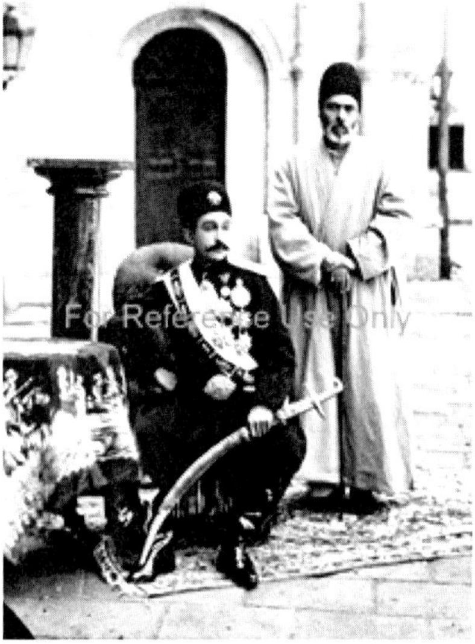

Figure 5: Photographer: Antoin Sevruguin.

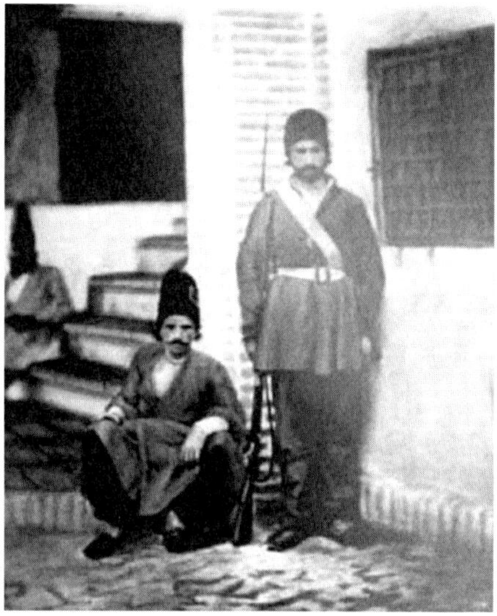

Figure 6: Niavaran Palace guards, 1862, Luigi Montabone (photographer), Golestan Palace Photo Gallery, Album 374/7395.

portraits taken by the king himself, who, in a number of cases, produced creative photographs.

In certain other cases, however, the shah's work was merely an imitation of the pornographic images being made in European studios. Later, such photographs were imitated by women from aristocratic families and, by the end of the Qajar dynasty, by middle-class women (Tahmasbpour, 2002). No foreign photographer photographed the king's courtesans as such individuals were not permitted in the king's harem; they were only allowed to depict the men and children.

Photographs of ordinary women are divided into two main categories: unveiled women shot indoors, in the studios and mansions of aristocrats and noblemen, and photographs taken outdoors, in the streets, public places, mosques and shrines (Talayi 2008). Women's clothing differed according to the setting. In studios and indoors, women are clothed with Iranian garments. These photographs were created by both Iranian and foreign photographers.

The photographs of women outdoors primarily were made by foreign

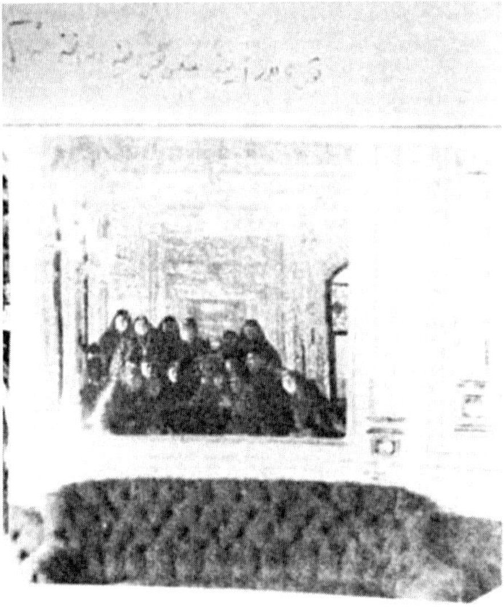

Figure 7: Inside the Mirror Hall, Nasser al-Din Shah (photographer), Golestan Palace Photo Gallery.

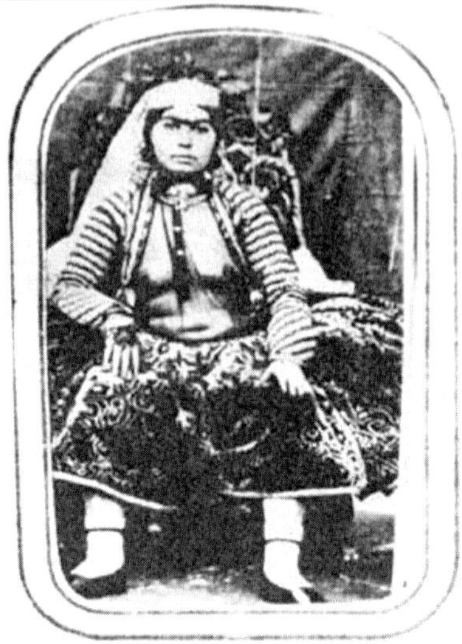

Figure 8: One of Nasser al-Din Shah's harem wives, Nasser al-Din Shah (photographer).

photographers, as they could not photograph the women in closed environments such as houses. These photographs indicate the social spaces in which women were allowed.

Another interesting point is the way in which women of religious minorities were dressed. As Delrisch (1996) states, the outfits worn by women of religious minorities were different from those worn by Muslim women. Leaving home, Armenian women had to wear a white, long, simple veil, made of soft fabric, down to their wrists. They veiled their mouths and noses with a soft, thin fabric so that they would not be recognized.

Prostitutes and Dancers

Albeit unauthorized and illegal, prostitutes and dancers continued to work during the Qajar era without any practical restrictions. Yet the religious sanctions that encouraged Iran's traditional society not to acknowledge these groups of women turned photographers away from them.

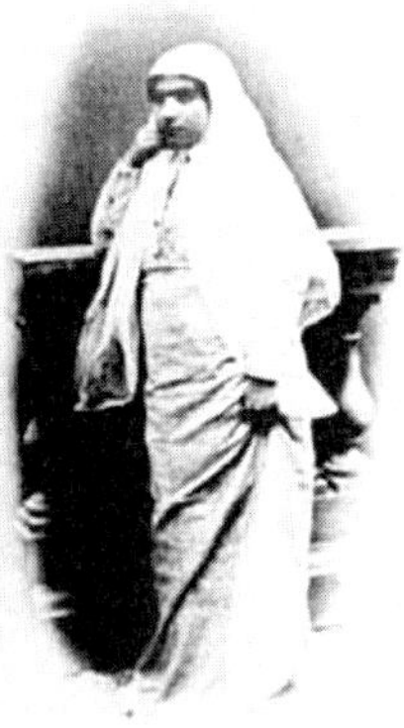

Figure 9: A lady in a private studio, anonymous photographer.

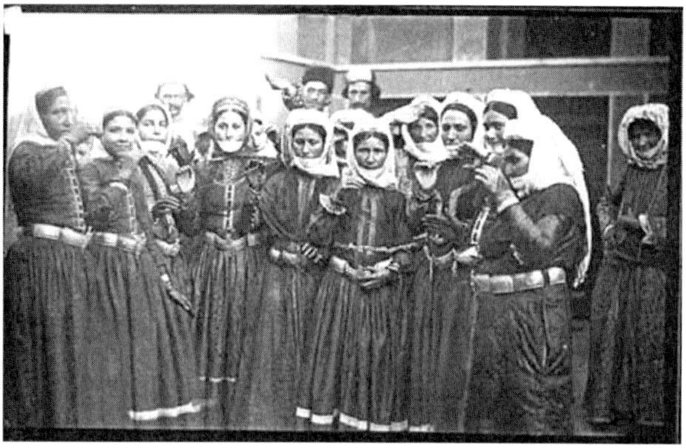

Figure 10: Armenian women, Ernest Holster (photographer).

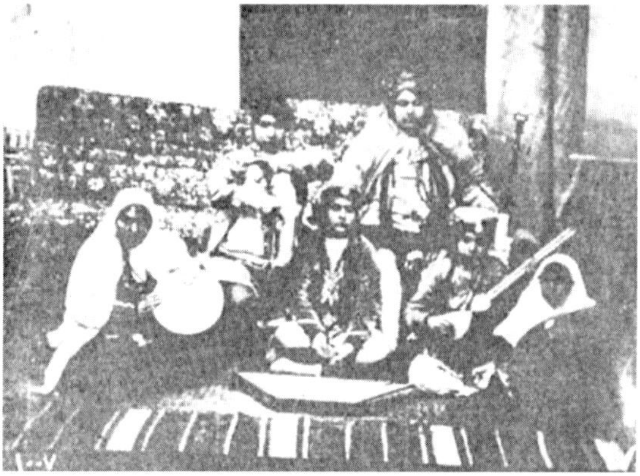

Figure 11: Golin Majeure, University of Tehran Central Library.

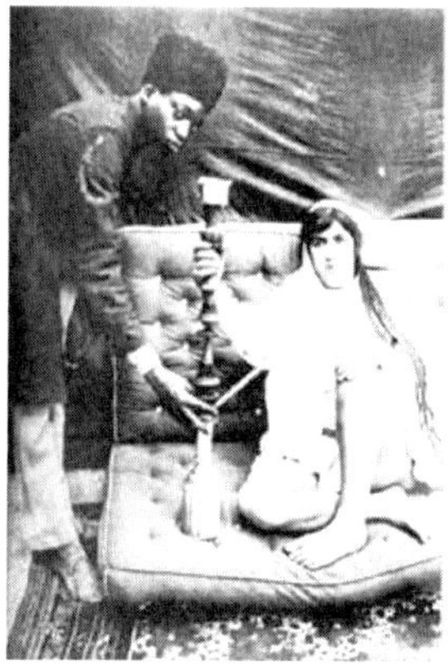

Figure 12: Photographer: Antoin Sevruguin.

However, some photographers selected them as models to represent oriental assumptions about Eastern women. In some books, these outcasts are presented as Iranian women.

Although Suvruigin's photographs originated from reality, the romantic approach in his staged photographs seeks to evoke exoticism, which has turned them into non-documentary or even unreal images (Sheikh 1999). Another form of this approach was depicting women in men's clothing.

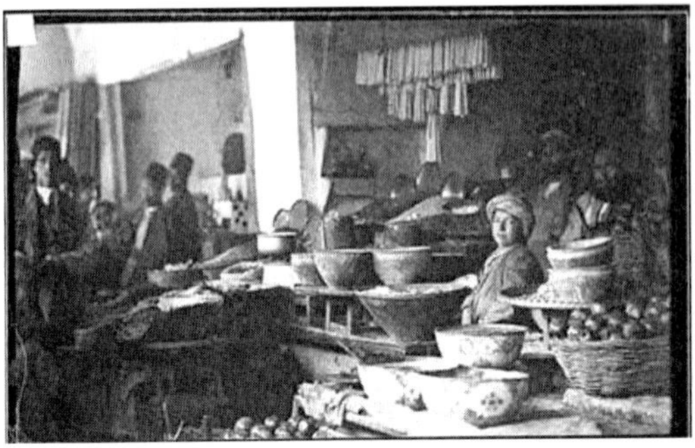

Figure 13: Photographer: Ernest Holster.

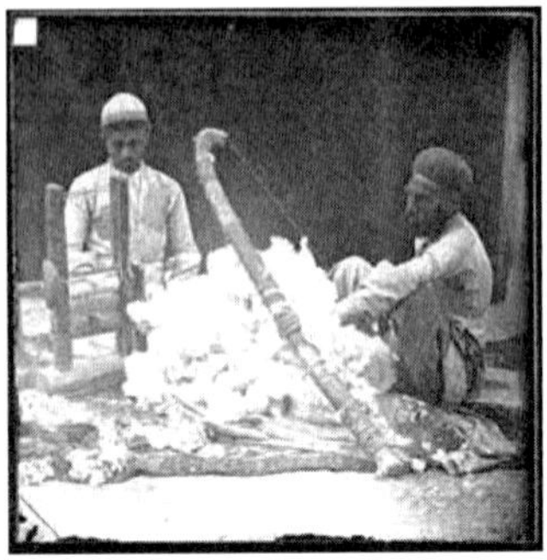

Figure 14: Photographer: Ernest Holster.

Bazaars and workshops

Most Eastern artisans work in bazaars. Traditional, conventional bazaars existed in both open-air and indoor environments. A bazaar seems to be composed of different social groupings. As a result, photographers explored bazaars as sociologists and highlighted interesting human relations. Iranian photographers' small share of photographs capturing bazaars and workshops indicates that they were not interested in the issue. Instead, foreign photographers, recognizing the bazaar's rich potential for providing documentary themes and subjects, began taking pictures of different occupations, passers-by, customers and salesmen. Holster is among the photographers who compiled a very detailed list of Isfahan's occupations and professions as well as photographing them.

Iranian ethnic groups

Ethnicity is another form of anthropological categorization that can be explored extensively in Iran due to the country's ethnic diversity. Iranian photographers, often commissioned by the kings, took photographs of different parts of the country. Photographing Iranian ethnicities was rarely done in a purposeful way, as Iranian photographers only took photographs of the tribes' elders and wealthy people.

On the other hand, foreign photographers adopted an ethnographic approach and tried to portray Iran's social context. Accordingly, they shot

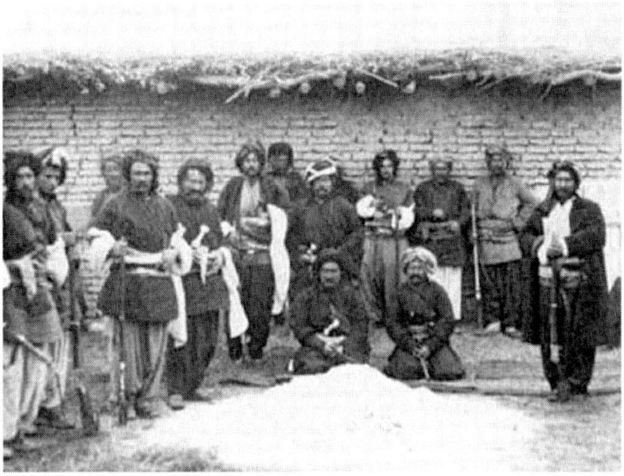

Figure 15: Local people in Hooratash, Sardasht, Ali Khan Hakem (photographer).

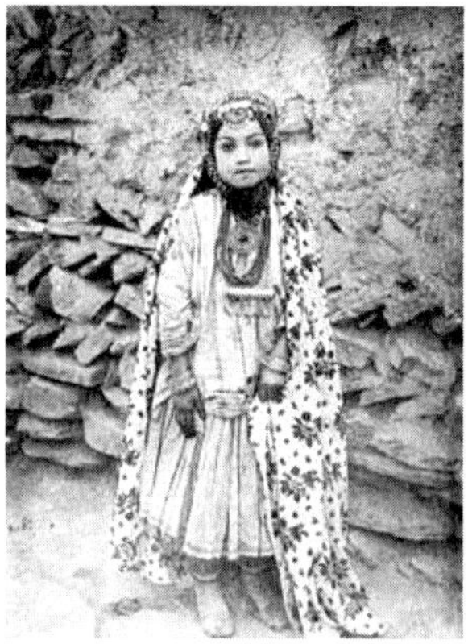

Figure 16: Photographer: Antoin Sevruguin.

people in real-life contexts. As Stein (1989) describes, Iranians' lifestyle is increasingly changing, with luxurious and glamorous European lifestyles mediating Iranian customs in the last few years, and, gradually, many traditions, architecture and even the way people dress would be thoroughly eliminated – nothing of what Chardin and Tavarnieh had described would survive.

Prisoners and convicts

Representing criminals in photographic images was appreciated by the royal court. As a result of various political urges, the authorities had convicts photographed. Thus, in the Qajar period, there was a close relationship between photographers and authorities. In his last years on the throne, Nasser al-Din Shah commissioned Muhammad Hassan Khan Qajar to photograph Qazvin prisoners, including Haj Muhammad Ali Mahalati, Mirza Reza Kirmani, and Haj Ali Amin Shahizadi (Zoka 1997).

Most of the photographs taken by foreign photographers are public scenes, such as executions or convicts being tortured. The photographers might have intended to depict Easterners as violent people.

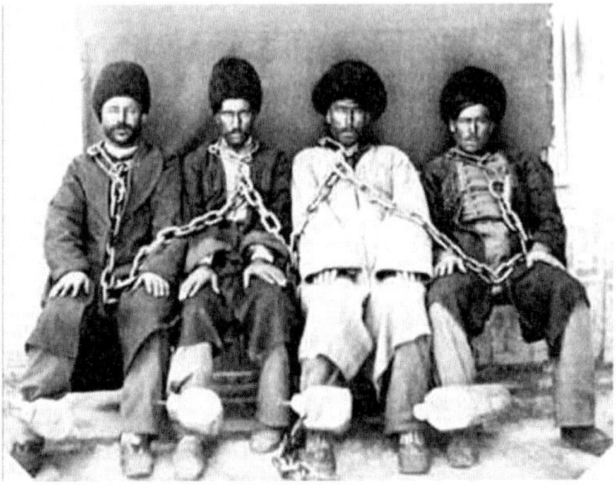

Figure 17: Photographer: Agha Reza ʿakkasbashi.

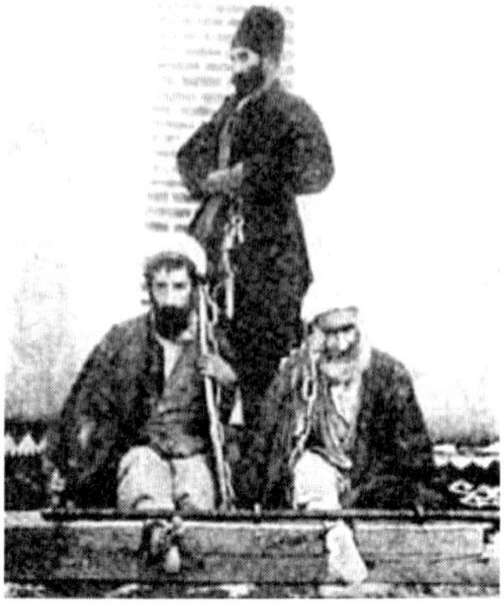

Figure 18: Mirza Reza Kermani and Haj Sayah Mahalati in custody, anonymous photographer.

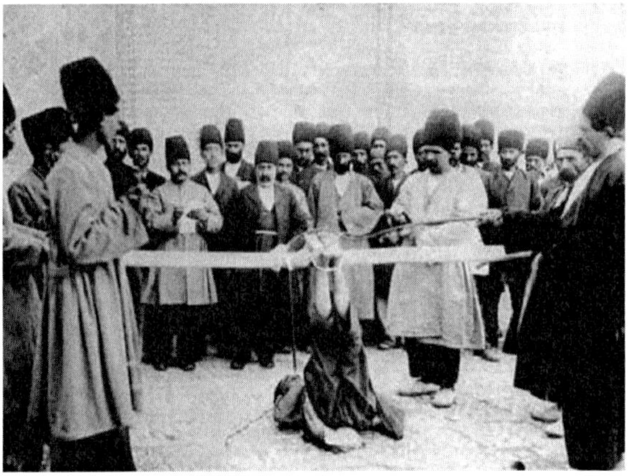

Figure 19: Photographer: Antoin Sevruguin.

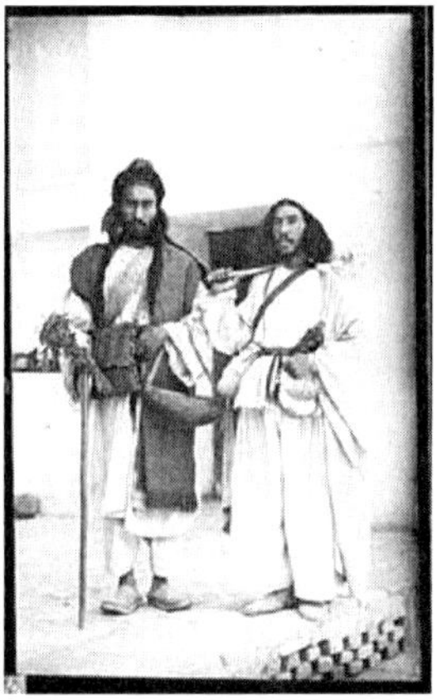

Figure 20: Photographer: Ernest Holster.

Beggars and Darvishes

In the Eastern and Iranian context, beggars and darvishes are recognized as a legitimate guild. Coexisting with other classes of society, they were not treated as outcasts. However, Iranian photographers rarely took pictures of beggars and darvishes because, as photographers commissioned by the royal court, they viewed these people as too inferior to be recorded. On the

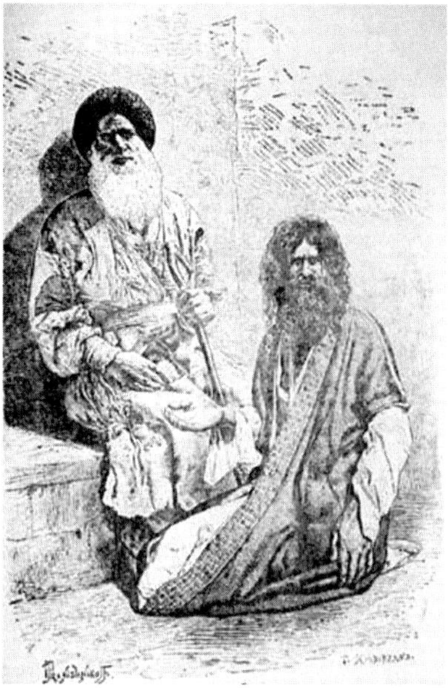

Figure 21: Bassmeh, Madame Jean Diolafou (photographer).

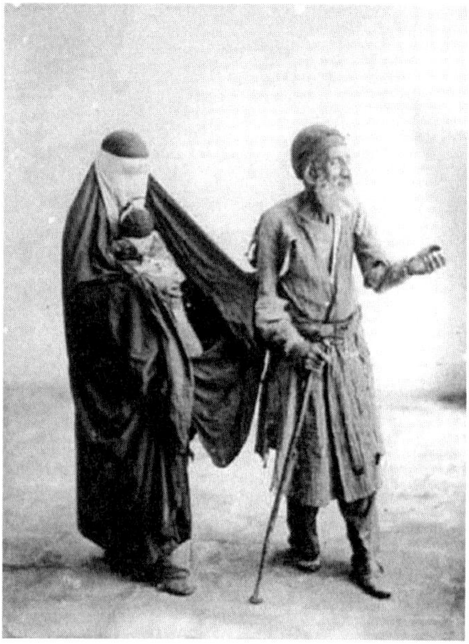

Figure 22: A beggar, Antoin Sevruguin (photographer).

other hand, beggars and darvishes were not a common sight for Westerners, and, in line with their oriental assumptions, foreign photographers paid much attention to these seemingly inferior people. To these photographers, the attire, figures and belongings of these people were unique subjects, and these two groups were photographed by most of the foreign photographers who travelled to Iran.

In some cases, these groups of people were photographed in studios, where they were subject to exaggeration.

Clerics

Religion, a key factor in Iranin history, is represented by clerics. This group is a hierarchal one, from protégé to philosopher. Clerics play a key role in religious, social and political affairs and are highly respected. Iranian photographers have depicted clerics preaching, teaching and in other real-life contexts. These images were intended to attract the clerics' approval of pho-

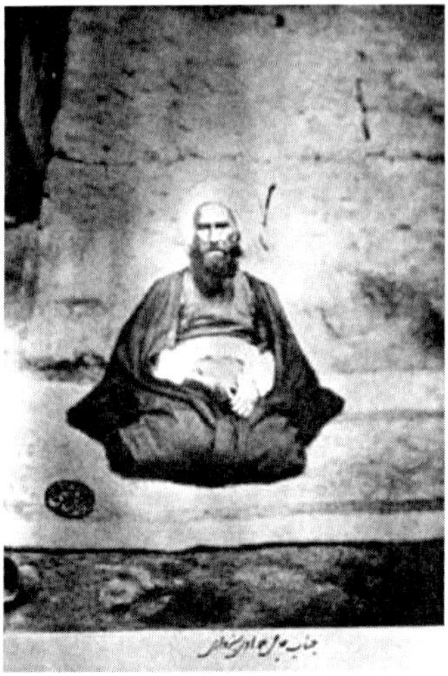

Figure 23: Haji Mulla Hadi Sabzivari, Agha Reza ʿakkasbashi (photographer), 1866, Album 142, Golestan Palace Photo Gallery.

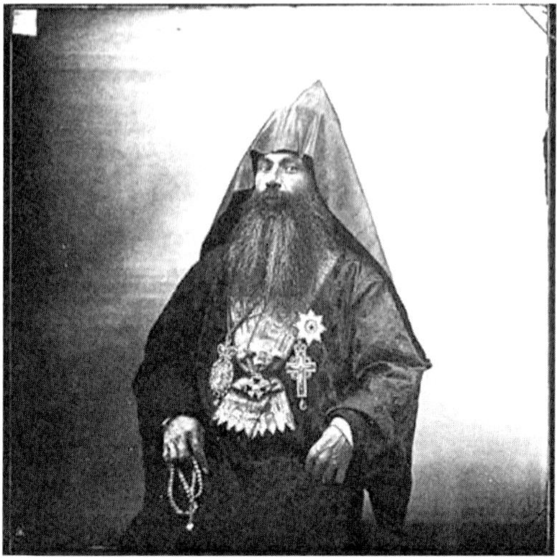

Figure 24: Christian priest, Ernest Holster (photographer).

tography. Agha Reza ʿakkasbashi was commissioned by the king to travel to Khorasan and photograph the senior philosopher and cleric Hakim Mulla Hadi Sabzivari. As Agha Reza Akasbahsi photographed the renowned figure, Mulla Hadi was quite astonished, never having seen the process of photography and regarding it as a violation of religious rules (Tahmasbpour 1990). Not being Muslims, Western photographers could rarely make their way into clerics' private lives and spaces. However, Suvruigin photographed clerics in his studio.

Religious minorities

Among important factors of distinction in Iranian society, one might point to religion. Religious distinctions would manifest social differences or discriminations, which include clothing and architecture as well as religious rituals and even food and drink.

Iranian photographers were less concerned with minorities. One might think that not being allowed to enter their lives was a strong reason. Accordingly, most of the remaining images have been taken by foreign photographers. The early photographs are mostly portraits. The portraits of Christian leaders or priests by Sevruigin or Holster might draw the beholder to the conclusion that the photographs were copies of European portraits. This implies that the Western photographer pursued the interweaving of a subject in an Eastern setting with a Western notion.

Concluding remarks

Exploring issues as gender, profession and ethnicity, this chapter sought to highlight the considerable differences between Iranian and foreign photographers concerning equipment, vision, purposes and creativity. That is to say that Iranian photographers, enjoying the live experience they had in Iran's social context, have either proved to be more successful than their foreign counterparts or had more options for photography. On the other hand, regarding visual literacy and aesthetic and artistic features, foreign photographers outpaced their Iranian peers.

Browsing Iranian photographers' images, one would find these points as being significant: most Iranian photographers were born to aristocratic or royal families; they were titled by the king as *ʿakkasbashi*; as employees, they were compelled to handle their photographic careers according to the king's will; the creativity evident in the works of early Iranian photographers was not maintained by others; portraits taken in Iranian studios look like portraits produced by European photographers; lacking a strong, deep-rooted visual tradition, Iranian photographers were mostly trained by foreign photographers; for a long time, photography has been regarded as a means of entertainment and amusement; and documentary photographic series were commissioned by the king and freelance photographers did not go any further.

On the other hand, foreign photographers produced images with particular features, as they travelled to Iran to fulfil specific purposes. Some photographers accompanied political representatives; focused on the king, courtiers and the hierarchical power structure; and, consequently, made photographic series of courtiers, palaces, castles and armies. Another group, working in more independent modes, explored Iran's multi-layered social structure. This group of photographers, taking pictures of all social classes and strata, produced the greatest number of anthropological documentary photographs and, in the case of prohibitions and restrictions, pursued their photographic ideas in studios. Accordingly, some of their images are unreal and romantic, having an oriental function.

A thorough exploration of Iranian and foreign photographers' images would lead one to notice that the subject (Iranian people) is regarded as the 'other'. Considering cultural, financial and socioeconomic disparities as well as the patron's expectation – and failing to recognize the value of photography as a means of documenting society – Iranian photographers have looked through the different layers of society. The royal court employed photography as a means to highlight the gap between courtiers and the nation. The images of criminals, servants and maids or ceremonial occasions taken by Iranian photographers seem to imply the superiority of the royal court. As a result of economic and cultural reasons, people were never provided with photographic equipment in order to be portrayed through images. If people had photographed themselves, those images could have been compared with selected photographs of Iranian photographers.

As an explorer, the foreign photographer arrived in exotic Iran seeking new, fresh subjects. Highlighting social, religious and ethnic features, such photographers tried to depict Iran as different, outlandish and fascinating. Numerous anthropological images, as well as photographs taken from historical constructions and Iranian architecture, symbolize their astonishment and approval. However, regarding images of Iranian people, one might notice the Western preoccupation with portraying Iran as part of a mystical East. Subjects such as vulnerable social classes (beggars and darvishes who were a most readily available scene in the economically poor Iran of the Qajar era) or women in both documentary and staged settings have been represented according to Western ideas and assumptions. Foreign photographers, therefore, exploring these subjects, produced images representing poverty, misery and misfortune. Women, who probably constituted half of Iran's population in the Qajar period, were represented wearing exotic dresses and veils or in unreal, grotesque and bizarre places. These images intensified the Western orientalist approach to Iranians and, naturally, resulted in a distorted, misrepresented portrait of Iranians living in the Qajar era.

As stated earlier, photography and sociology were born simultaneously. Realizing the significance of images in anthropological studies, Western academies employed images to study societies, including Western societies. Accordingly, photographers were encouraged to photograph various subjects. Thus, art and knowledge began to explore humanity, and different social classes were examined. Foreign photographers, either intending to produce visual anthropological series for their countries or trying to find a market, explored Iran's multi-layered society and its subjects. However, lacking a scientific or sociological perspective, photographers of the Qajar era produced images merely to enrich personal and state archives. That is, photography was handled as means of entertainment and amusement. It is not surprising therefore, that the Iranian photographer has never been involved with his own society.

Back in the picture: early film techniques used to capture the Qajar era[1]

Alex Fischer

Introduction

The motion picture frame is more than a mere border, and within the confines of each celluloid rectangle lies a plane in which stories are told, events documented and agendas realized. The attention-grabbing power of a projected image has tremendous influence upon audience members. Yet, the typical viewer gives little thought as to the decisions dictating each shot and the subtext of the cinematography.

Modern cinematography is a language in which shot sizes, angles and camera movements communicate what is important to the viewer. The purpose of this cinematic language is to avoid audience confusion and to heighten the visualisation of the subject. So, as film production author Joseph Mascelli explains, 'the close-up may transport the viewer *into* the scene; *eliminate* all *non-essentials*, for the moment; and *isolate* whatever *significant* incident should receive narrative emphasis' (1965, p. 173).

The conventions of cinematic language, such as those associated with the close-up, have gradually evolved since the introduction of the first film camera in 1895. Interestingly, there are no hard and fast rules stipulating which type of shot size or camera angle must be employed for particular types of scenes. Rather, the techniques used to form the visual narrative

1 The author would like to thank Dr. Pedram Khosronejad and the Soudavar Memorial Foundation for their support of this project. Additional thanks are extended to Alexandra Shakhnazarova for her excellent translation services and to Dr. Alex Marlow-Mann for his suggestions and comments regarding the presentation of this information.

are at the discretion of the cinematographer, director, camera operator, producer, etc.

This chapter explores the cinematic language used to capture the Qajar dynasty. More specifically, it considers how both British and Russian motion picture cameras filmed important moments involving Qajar royalty and government officials. The goal of this investigation is to explore the possibility of political bias in the kinds of cinematic techniques used by both the British Empire and Soviet Russia when visually documenting their Persian counterparts.

The present text is based on an investigation into the surviving material on the Qajar era in two prominent European film archives, British Pathé and the Russian State Film and Photo Archive at Krasnogorsk (RGAKFD).[2] The information in this chapter is based on two films which will be discussed in-depth: 'Shah of Persia Inspects British Ship' and 'Signing a Peaceful Treaty between the USSR and Persia'.[3] These films were selected because both document important diplomatic events that took place around the same time.[4]

The conclusions reached in the pages ahead are based upon the author's experience as a filmmaker and lecturer on film production. That said, it is important to note that the kind of analysis conducted in this essay always involves subjective judgments. This problem is even greater for films of the early period because we have little contextual evidence about the production to support or disprove a hypothesis.

Unlike their contemporary counterparts, the pioneering camera operators, cinematographers and directors did not have set standards or precursors as to how cinematic language should be used. No doubt photography provided some basis for framing, but the aspect of movement was new and presented numerous possibilities that surpassed those of the still image. Similarly, much of the footage is not credited and it is difficult to ascertain whether there was a director or visual coordinator present, deliberately

---

2 This project was made possible through the generous support of the Soudavar Memorial Foundation.

3 Translated from Russian: 'Подписание мирного договора СССР с Персией'.

4 'Shah of Persia inspects British ship' (1918); 'Signing a peaceful treaty between the USSR and Persia' (unknown but thought to be 1921).

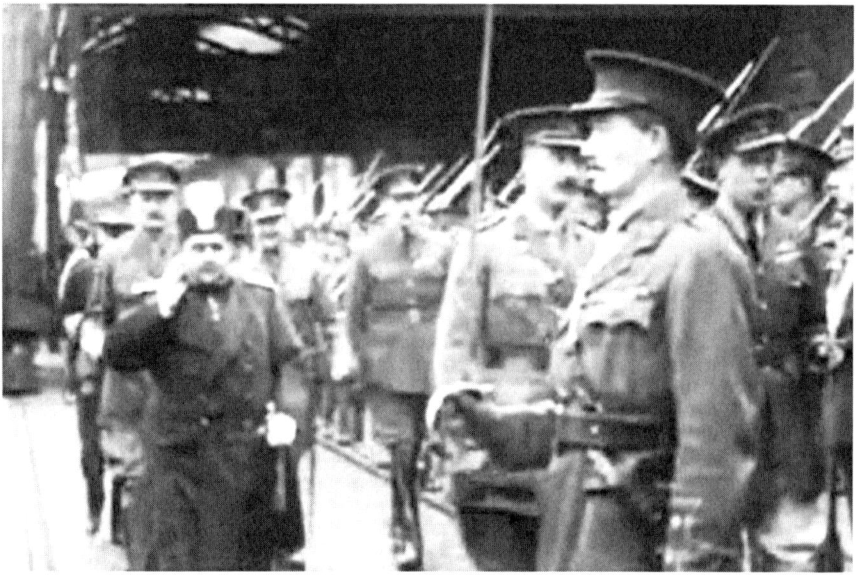

Figure 1

controlling the filming process and making aesthetically or ideologically motivated decisions or the footage was simply shot by a camera operator making purely practical decisions about how best to capture and record on film the events taking place.

We are therefore forced to rely simply on the (often incomplete) archival material available to us, drawing conclusions from what we see and grounding them, as far as possible, in knowledge of early film technology and the ways it was employed as well as the broader geo-political agendas at play at this particular historical juncture.

It is important to understand that the films under discussion were created shortly before the end of the Qajar dynasty in 1925. Thus, the respective relationships between Qajar and both Britain and Russia were fully developed by this time and had long histories that included wars, peace treaties, trade partnerships and even, to some extent, carried imperialistic overtones. In short, the backstory of these countries constitute a script itself worthy of film and, like any good story, there is an enthralling plot twist that adds to the drama: Britain and Russia were expansionist rivals.

The geographical location of Persia positioned the country as a site in which the colonial empires of Britain and Russian would collide on many fronts (Kazemzadeh 2013). While no direct references to the 'other' state are made in either film, the documenting of such interactions undoubtedly also intersected with political agendas.

Focusing specifically on the concept of political agendas reveals a significant distinction between British and Russian cinematography techniques. The majority of the British footage contains framing and camera angles that indicate a presumed superiority over and humiliation of the Qajar subjects, while the greater portion of the Russian footage viewed portrays its Persian subject with more respect.

It is possible that the difference between the two types of cinematography derives from a variation in the intended audience. That is to say, the footage found in the Pathé archive is newsreel in nature and thus its audience was most likely the British public, while the films in the RGAKFD seem to be for private, government-affiliated viewers. All of the films surveyed are silent, so narration of the images was limited to title and intertitle cards, many of which were not present in the extant Russian prints.

Signing a peaceful treaty between the USSR and Persia

One film that lacked any such titling but captured an important diplomatic moment was 'Signing a Peaceful Treaty between the USSR and Persia'. This film has no listed production date, but research indicates that it is footage of the signing of the treaty between the Russian Soviet government and Persia in Moscow on 26 February 1921. This date is of particular importance because the terms of the treaty were agreed upon before Reza Khan launched the military coup that would ultimately mark the end of the Qajar dynasty.

The notable Qajar official in this film is Mostowfi ol-Mamalik (1874–1932), former prime minister of Persia. Other Qajar diplomats are also present but cannot be identified. The noteworthy Soviet figures include Georgy Chicherin (1872–1936), People's Commissar for Foreign Affairs, and Lev Mikhailovich Karakhan (1889–1937), who at the time had recently served as the Deputy People's Commissar for Foreign Affairs.

What is most striking about this film is the use of varying shot sizes and multiple camera angles to document the event visually. For example, a mid-shot of Mostowfi ol-Mamalek will cut to a close-up of his face. The use of such scene dissection provides the viewer with a comprehensive presentation of the event.

Multiple continuity errors, such as sudden jumps in an individual's position when an edit occurs, suggest that the film was shot with a single camera. Similarly, there are numerous orphan frames, indicating that the edit is not a final product but rather a rough assemblage of the footage.

The respect shown to the Qajar representatives is apparent throughout the film. Most noticeable is the sense of balance. The framing sees three Qajar diplomats sitting across the table from their three Russian counterparts. Head and shoulder shots in which specific individuals look directly into the camera lens are set at eye-level, conveying a sense of equality. It is also interesting to note that close-ups are used to highlight key Russian and Qajar individuals. The same close-up shot used to distinguish Lev Mikhailovich Karakhan is used to frame Mostowfi ol-Mamalek. Such equality of framing leaves the viewer with the impression that a common ground has been reached and the two parties are on equal footing.

It is quite probable that the action was deliberately (re-)staged for the camera. The extensive coverage of the scene would have been extremely difficult to shoot with a single camera simply because moving the camera to a new position would have meant missing a part of the document signing. Similarly, the progression of shots gives rise to the notion that this production was specifically engineered. For example, a mid-shot of Mostowfi ol-Mamalik signing the peace agreement is immediately followed by a close-up of his hand penning his signature. Such coverage, as already stated, gives the viewer a comprehensive and intimate view of the action. There are also candid moments in which individuals can be seen communicating directly with the camera operator. In such instances the operator seems to be suggesting actions, such as a tilting of the head or even the odd smile.

Throughout the entire film there is only one camera movement, a single and somewhat jerky pan. The majority of shots are therefore static, and the framing is deliberate and concentrates on specific details of the scene: Georgy Chicherin studying the document, a handshake between Mostowfi ol-Mamalik and Lev Mikhailovich Karakhan, wax being melted for the stamping of an official seal.

Given the turbulent and often conflict-ridden past between Russia and the Qajar dynasty, this film presents images representative of a strong and committed alliance between the two countries. We can speculate that such a deliberate use of cinematography was intended to send a message the British, given that this particular treaty followed the failed Anglo-Persian Agreement of 1919.

Shah of Persia inspects British ship

The film titled 'Shah of Persia Inspects British Ship' presents the opposite picture with regard to the equality and balance demonstrated in the Russian film. As previously mentioned, the majority of the British material viewed conveys an overarching feeling of superiority over its Qajar subjects. This superiority is evident from, and primarily driven by, the militaristic nature of these newsreel clips.

According to the archive notes, this particular film was shot between 1914 and 1918 and coincided with Ahmad Shah (1898–1930) Qajar's visit to the United Kingdom.[5] The film itself is very simple in structure: three linearly edited shots. What is most striking is the framing of the image, which places the Shah between the military might of the British (soldiers with rifles, the superstructure of an HMS battleship, etc.) and the hard black edge of the film's frame. For example, in the opening shot Ahmad Shah is seen walking toward the camera. To his left (camera right) stands a formidable wall of British soldiers, all at attention with rifles and fixed bayonets. The danger imposed by the British military is heightened by the left edge of the film frame, to which the Shah walks precariously close, at times almost straying out of shot.

This scene leaves the impression that the Shah is caught between two powerful and potentially dangerous elements: the British and oblivion. This position is heightened as the Shah draws closer to the camera and is forced to step around a British solder holding a sword. The unflinching posture of

---

5 It is likely that this film was produced during 1919, as this was the only time the Shah is known to have visited the UK.

the solder and the physical difference in stature between the two individuals presents the Shah as a weaker individual. Similarly, the rigid and straight lines displayed by the British military are in stark contrast to the open palm salute and roundish figure of the Shah.

The camera is mounted on a tripod at a height equal to that of the Shah's gaze. Again, the physical stature of the British men in the scene gives the impression of power, as the solders' eyelines are all above the camera lens, so that the Shah (and the viewer) must look up into the face of this imposing force. Such a camera position reinforces the impression that the British are in a position of power.

The scene depicts the Shah following the steps of Prince Albert (1819–1861) and a high-ranking British officer. The Shah is trailed by five British officers and therefore is completely surrounded by the British, without any other Qajar officials in sight. This is in stark contrast to the balance displayed by the Russian film.

The second shot differs significantly from the first in that it is from an elevated position, and thus the viewer looks down on both the Shah and his British hosts. Additionally, the military pomp that dominated the first scene has given way to a more relaxed assembly of British troops. Whereas previously the British seemed to squeeze the Shah through their stiff posture, they now appear more to be curious observers forgoing any formal salutes or tributes to his authority in order simply to gawk at his passing.

The Shah no longer has his hand raised in salute and seems to be walking at a more relaxed pace as he moves toward the gangway of a battleship. Unlike in the previous scene, two other Persian dignitaries accompany him. As soon as the Shah reaches the midpoint of the frame the camera begins to pan, following his movement. In a moment of spontaneity he stops to salute the British officer standing at the top of gangway; the officer appears somewhat surprised by the Shah's actions and twice bows his head. This is the first personalized sign of respect evident in this scene. The shot ends with the Shah stepping onto the battleship, only to be swallowed by ship's superstructure.

The third and final shot lasts only a few seconds and shows the Shah standing at the aft of the vessel. He stands alone, but British soldiers are scattered around the deck. The camera's elevated position is from the same vantage point as the previous shot, the only difference being that the camera has been rotated to the right and now frames the ship. There are no clear shots of the Shah, and throughout the entire scene he is obscured by the ship or its equipment. The significance of this final shot is unclear, as what is occurring on the ship is impossible to discern.

This footage does not present the Shah's authority in a positive fashion. Rather, the viewer is more likely to be impressed by the power of the British military. An additional point of interest is the relationship between Prince Albert, who led the inspection of the ship, and the Shah. There are no instances that indicate any sort of connection or respect. Instead, the Shah appears to be following the Prince without interaction. The constructed nature of the scene means that the filmmaker may have deemed that depicting such interaction was unnecessary (or ideologically counterproductive) and therefore the action was never filmed or was edited out of the final film.

It is important to note that the timing of this production coincides with the First World War (1914–1918), a period in which British-Persian relations were strained due to British use of Persian territory to fight the Ottoman Empire. The framing and shot composition in the film are not indicative of friendly relations but rather a reminder of who holds the bigger stick in the relationship. This is in stark contrast to the previously discussed Russian film and gives rise to the hypothesis that the cinematic language employed was intended to serve a particular ideological function.

This chapter has suggested that the particular cinematic techniques used to capture images of the Qajar dynasty may have been the product of particular political agendas. Obviously we have no contextual evidence as to the filmmakers' political intentions (production notes, filmmakers' interviews, etc.) and thus are forced to rely on close textual analysis, deciphering the political agenda from the formal characteristics of extant archival films.

This essay should be considered only a first step toward an understanding of the visual representational strategies used by the British and Russians toward the Qajar dynasty, and the topic merits further investigation for several reasons. First, funding only allowed the author to investigate two archives and it is extremely probable that numerous films featuring Qajar subjects exist in other European film archives. Most of these films are unknown to Qajar experts, and additional or even new information likely would be gained by identifying and studying these films. Second, film is a powerful medium that provides a literal recording of events as they transpire (rather than a verbal transcription). For this reason, subjective decisions on the part of the filmmaker as to which kinds of cinematic technique to employ are particularly revealing of ideological or political agendas. Such an analysis can therefore better reveal the kind of image a particular country is trying to project and how this interacts with the foreign policy being pursued at the time. Finally, this paper is only one example of the insights that can be gained from an examination of the ways in which imperialistic nations portray their subjects though cinema.[6] As mentioned, both Russia and Britain had vested interests in Persia and Qajar politics. The cinemagraphic subtext of 'tit-for-tat' types of filmmaking illuminates an interesting aspect of colonial expansionism – in this case, the chess game played by both nations and the efforts they expended when attempting to capture the Qajar dynasty.

[6] Other recent examples include Lee Grieveson and Colin MacCabe (eds), *Empire and Film* and *Film and the End of Empire* (both London: BFI/Palgrave MacMillan, 2011).

Portraiture in Qajar Iran and the Ottoman Empire: a comparative approach

Başak Kilerci

Years ago, I found a photograph of my eighty-five-year-old grandfather, taken eighty years earlier (fig. 1). His mother sits, surrounded by her two sons, looking directly at the camera. She is wearing a long dress and a kind of *fez*; the two boys are wearing long dresses named *entari.* When I asked my grandfather about this photograph he told that his mother was very excited to pose for the camera. She had invited a photographer to the house and asked her sons not to tell their father about it. A naughty child, my grandfather, as soon as his father returned, told him that they had posed for a camera. His father said, 'Muslim women do not pose for the camera; photographing the human being is forbidden in Islam'. He burned the photos, but this example remained.

This story always reminds me of the cliché that 'human imagery is forbidden in Islam' and the art historical debate around the art of portraiture. In her article 'Theory and practice of portraiture in Persian tradition', Soucek discusses different opinions about and interpretations of portraiture in the Islamic world. Papadopoulo (cited in Soucek 2000, p. 97) claims that there were never to be portraits in Muslim art, while Arnold (*ibid* 2000, p. 98) identifies any representation of a princely figure as a portrait. On the other hand, Richard Brilliant (*ibid* 2000, p. 97) defines portraiture as a cultural construct, depicting living or once-living people. For Soucek, however, what defines a portrait as a portrait is not the 'individualized' or 'Western-style' aspect. An image can be viewed as a portrait if contemporary viewers recognize it as the depiction of a specific person and it evokes

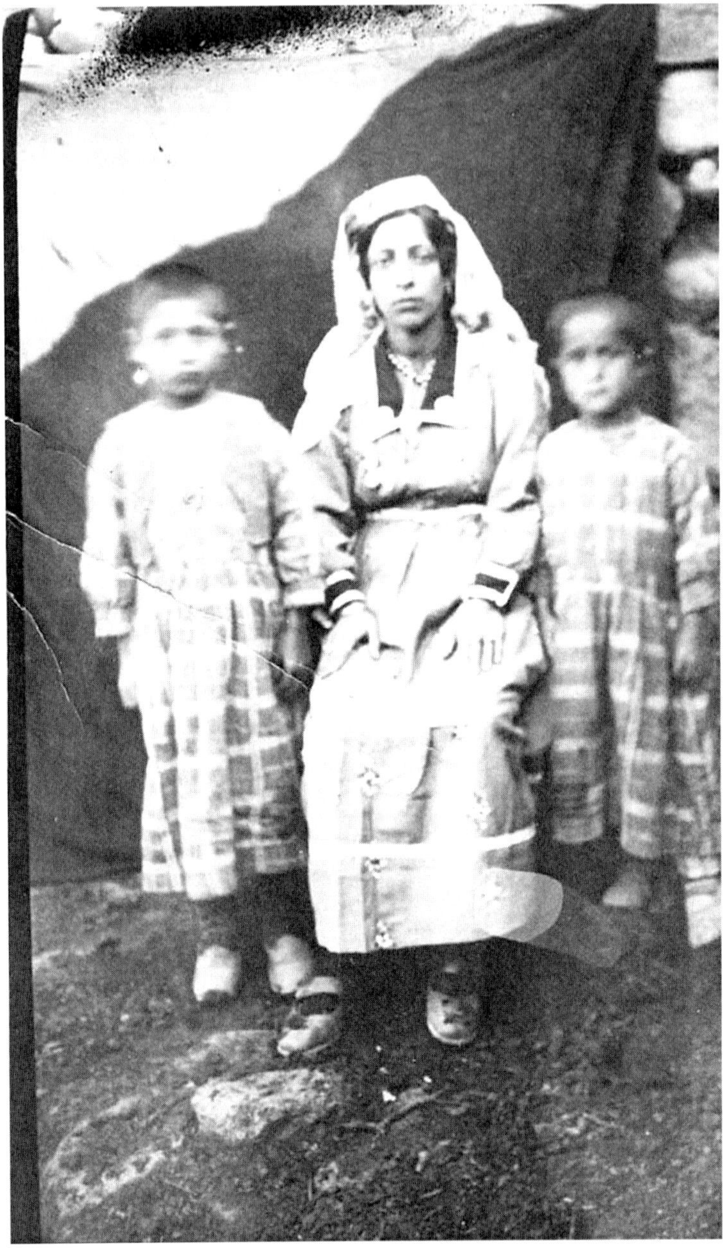

Figure 1

a memory of that person. In other words, what makes a portrait is not that it precisely reflects 'reality', but what it reflects within a social and historical context. So, 'when a local tradition describes something as a portrait, it must be understood how that type of portraiture functioned and which aspects of the culture might have nurtured and encouraged its development' (*ibid* 2000, p. 98).

Both Iran and the Ottoman Empire have a long history of portraiture. As Soucek mentions (*ibid* 2000, p. 104), there is a practice of linking an author's portrait with his text in the twelfth century; portrait-like paintings on the opening pages of a manuscript became popular in the fifteenth century. Only in the eighteenth century, however, did painting (portraits) came out of the page and onto the canvas. Previously, portraits were placed on rock reliefs and coinage and appeared as illustrations in manuscripts. From eighteenth century on, with the influences of westernization, a change in the production and education of art, including the tradition of portraiture, appears both in Iran and in the Ottoman Empire.

In Iran during the Timurid (1370–1507) and Safavid (1501–1736) eras, artists were trained in the royal *kitabkhana*. In the first half of the nineteenth century artistic activities continued to be mainly limited to the *naqqaskhana*, but we know that traditional workshops called *karkhana* and palace-based workshops called *Buyutat-i Saltanati* were also existent (Ekhtiar 1998, p. 51). In nineteenth-century Iran, many modern health, military and education services were formulated, and schools such as *Darolfonoon* (1851) and *Maktab-i Naqqashiy-i Majani* (Free Painting School, 1861) were founded. The *Darolfonoon* provided an education both in painting and in photography. It absorbed the *Maktab-i Naqqashiy-i Majani* in which painting classes previously had been held (Floor 1999, p. 131). Furthermore, *Darolfonoon* included two photography workshops. The first was solely for the needs of the palace, while the second was mainly for training artists and students (Afshar 1992, p. 266). In addition to these, Nasser al-Din Shah's famous photography studio, *ʿakskhana* (Floor 1999, p. 129), and *Takkiyih Dawlat*, in which *taʿzieh* performances were held, functioned as workshops for artists.

When we look at the Ottoman Empire, we see that miniature paintings were produced in the *nakkaşhane*, which is thought to have been within the palace grounds. It was a school and a workshop for painters with a strict hierarchy. Starting in the beginning of the eighteenth century that hierarchy gradually dissolved and a more westernized system was adopted for the training and production of arts. Fine arts classes in the Ottoman Empire were first introduced within the military schools. Founded by Selim III (1761–1808) in 1795, the *Mühendishane-i Hümayun* (Imperial Engineering School) was the first school of that kind. It provided an education in architecture and engineering; the students were also taught painting, to acquire technical drawing skills (Cezar 1995, p. 377). In the nineteenth-century Ottoman Empire the modernization process was rapidly advancing in the-*post-Tanzimat* period. During the reign of Sultan Abdülhamid II (1842–1918), modern education, health and military services were formulated; many museums, factories and art schools – such as the *Sanayi-i Nefise Mektebi* (1883), *Yıldız Çini Fabrika-i Hümayun* (1890) and the photography studio founded on Abdülhamid II's order within the Yıldız Palace – functioned as both workshops and schools for artists.

Discussing the influence of Westernization and modernization process on the art of portraiture, this paper explores the role of portraiture in representing the nineteenth-century Ottoman and Qajar image: 'traditional/historical' and 'modern/Western'. It aims to examine how painting and photographic portraiture was used by the Ottoman and Qajar states in re-creating the past and propagating dynastic power in order to legitimize or re-legitimize their official authority.

Qajar Iran

The Qajars, a Turcoman-kizilbash tribe that gained power in the eighteenth century, were trying to find dynastic and cultural roots as a way of legitimizing their power and authority by rooting themselves to a noble past. This effort had three basic dimensions: Nomadic, Islamic and pre-Islamic. Abbas Amanat (2008, p. 7) mentions these three dimensions but also adds a Western dimension to the major factors that shaped the Qajar political agenda in the nineteenth century.

First, the 'Nomadic concept' reveals itself in the titles that Qajar rulers used. Aqa Muhammed Khan (1742–1797) adopted the titles *khan* and *shah*.

By contrast, Fath ʿAli Shah (1772–1834), second ruler of the Qajar Dynasty, adopted not only the ancient Persian title of *Shahanshah* but also the Turco-Mongol title of *khaqan* (the *khan* of *khans*) (2008, p. 10). His grandson Nasser al-Din Shah (1831–1896) also used titles such as 'al-sultan al-aʿzam wa al-khaqan al-afkham' (the greatest sultan and the greatest khakan) and 'al sultan b. al sultan b. al sultan b. wa al-khaqan b. al-khaqan b. al-khaqan shahinshah Dhuʾl Qarnayn'. As Soucek (Soucek 2001, p. 68) argues, these titles stressed the importance of his ancestry while also invoking a title of Quranic origin: Dhuʾl Qarnayn, or Alexander the Great.

The Islamic dimension can be interpreted as a way to form a connection with the Safavids, especially in the early days of the Qajars, when they aimed to represent themselves as the dynastic and cultural inheritors of the Safavids. Fath ʿAli Khan, the ancestor of the Qajars, served as the commander in chief for the last of the Safavid shahs, Tahmasp II (1722–32) and Nadir Shah (1736–47), the founder of the Afsharid dynasty (1736–1749) (Amanat 1998, p. 15). Furthermore, the Qajars were using the Shiite identity of the Safavids. The manifestation of Shiite identity can be seen through the passion play commemorating Hussein's martyrdom, the *taʿzieh.* In Qajar Iran, *taʿzieh* was supported by the court and became very popular. A huge tradition of painting grew out of it, and specific structures were built for its performance (Peterson 1979, pp. 64–87). Nasser al-Din Shah supported *taʿzieh* performances and paintings, which can be considered visual manifestations of Shiite existence and power in Qajar Iran. During his reign a huge building named *Takkiyih Dawlat* was built for *taʿzieh* performances within the Golestan Palace Complex.

Moreover, Nasser al-Din Shah was very interested in the stories of *One Thousand and One Nights* and ordered a translation project of it during his years as a prince in Tabriz. Immediately after he ascended to the Qajar throne he ordered a huge illustration project of the *Nights*, directed by Sani al-Mulk (1778–1830) under the supervision of Prince Dust ʿAli Khan Muʿayyir al-Mamalik (1857–1913) (Semsar 2000, p. 223). These projects can be considered part of an attempt to refer to the 'golden ages' of Islam. Because it is not clear whether there were other Persian translations of the *Nights* before the nineteenth century, we can only guess that Nasser al-Din Shah's enthusiasm derives from the popularity of Galland's edition in Europe. Amanat discovered that the famous illustration from the *Nights* depicts Nasser al-Din Shah in place of Harun Rashid and his vizier Amir Kabir (1807–1852) in place of Harun Rasid's vizier Barmaki. This can be seen as an example of the Qajar attempt to increase their authority by referring to the Abbasid period, considered the 'golden age' of Islam (Amanat 1998, pp. 14–29). Although his interest in the *Nights* probably derived from a European edition, it is also possible that he recognized the Persian elements and motifs in the *Nights* when it was read to him. This could be one of the motivations for his quick decision to commission the illustration of the *Nights*. With this project, the Qajars were trying to 'Persianize' the stories through illustrations and make references not only to the Abbasid period and the 'golden age' of Islam but also to the ancient past of Iran.

Although the Qajars tried to depict themselves as the dynastic and cultural inheritors of the Safavids, their goal was to surpass the Safavids, reach into the ancient past – the third dimension that shaped the Qajar social and political agenda, and bring all of the elements of their near and distant past together. The *Kayanid* Crown, which was a creation of Aqa Muhammad Shah's time, is an example of this goal. It is a symbolic example that brings both ancient and Safavid past together, as the word *Kayani* is from the *Shahnama* of Firdawsi and its shape was nurtured by Safavids (Amanat 2001, p. 22). It has been considered a symbol of the royal authority of the Qajars, who were trying to find their ancient roots.

The Qajars were trying to create a dynastic and cultural lineage from Achemenids and Sasanians to their own time. Aqa Muhammad Khan used the title 'Iskandar-i Iran', which reminds one of the ancient past of Iran and equates Aqa Muhammad to Iskandar, a conqueror (Kashani Sabet 2001, p. 209). In addition, following the Golestan treaty, according to which Iran lost its southern territories, Iranians' tendency to mask their weakness with 'ceremonial pomp' – to use Soucek's term – also can be seen in Fath ʿAli Shah's coinage (Soucek 2001, p. 68). He continued to use the title 'sultan al sultan' and, according to Fasai, two new coins were issued. The silver coins were inscribed 'Fath ʿAli Shah Khusraw Sahib Qiran' and the gold ones 'Fath ʿAli Shah Khusraw-i Kishvar Sitan' (Soucek 2001, p. 68). Khusraw compares him to rulers from Iran's pre-Islamic past, and the title 'sahib qiran' evokes messianic ideas and the memory of Timur together with the

Mughal Emperor Akbar, who had used it among his titles (Soucek 2001, 68).

In addition to the titles that we see on his coinage, Fath ʿAli Shah was eager to legitimize his authority and to equate himself with the ancient rulers. He was trying to represent his power and authority through rock reliefs, as did the pre-Islamic rulers. For instance, he added his reliefs to the ancient ones in *Taq-i Bustan* (Diba, 1998, p. 32). Furthermore, *Shahanshahnama* (Book of the King of Kings),

[1] an epic intended to equate Qajar rulers with the heroes of Firdawsi's *Shahnama*, and the *Muraqqaʿ (album)*[2] – in which Fath ʿAli Shah sets himself together with heroes from the *Shahnama* and past conquering rulers of Iran, such as Shah Abbas I (1587–1629); Shah Abbas II (1642–66); Ismail I (1501–24), the founder of the Safavid dynasty; Nadir Shah (1688–1747), the founder of the Afsharid dynasty (1736–47); Karim Khan Zand (1705–1779), the founder of the Zand dynasty (1750–79) as well as Jamshid and Kay Kawus from *Shahnama* – were part of the effort to create a dynastic lineage of rulers from the ancient past to the Qajar period. This was not only revival of the past but also a rivalry with the past.

The Ottoman Empire

With regard to the Ottoman Empire, we can say that in the nineteenth century, there was a growing interest in medieval Islamic and Turkic history and a tendency to glorify earlier eras. For instance, Ziya Paşa (1825–1880), an intellectual of the *Tanzimat* period, wrote *Endülüs Tarihi* (The History of Andalusia), while Abdülhak Hamid (1852–1937), a famous Ottoman poet and writer, wrote many historical plays about Andalusia, such as *Tarık* and *Tezer*.[3] Namık Kemal (1840–1888), another famous figure of the *Tanzimat* period, wrote a novel entitled *Celaleddin Harzemşah* relating the life-story of a medieval Turkic king who fought against the non-Muslim Mongols. While works about Andalusia referred to the western- Islamic past, works

1 Diba mentions that his manuscript of *Shahanshahnama* has four copies sent by Fath ʿAli Shah to English, Russian and Australian rulers. See Diba and Ekhtiar 1998: p. 171.

2 For the manuscript, see Diba and Ekhtiar 1998: p. 176.

3 For more information on this topic, see: Enginün 2002.

dealing with the medieval Turkic world highlighted the eastern-Turkic Islamic past.

Selim Deringil (2002, p. 42) uses the word 'obsession' to define the Ottoman interest in their early years that was extensive during the Hamidian era. Tombs of the founder of Ottoman dynasty, Osman Bey, his son Orhan Bey, and his father *Ertuğrul* Gazi, who is known as the ancestor and mythical founder of the dynasty, were repaired, rebuilt and 're-invented' in the Hamidian era. Every year a ceremony called *ihtifal* took place in the mausoleum of *Ertuğrul* (2002, p. 41). Moreover, to reinforce the significance of the mosque of *Ertuğrul*, other buildings that surround the mosque were destroyed. In an annual ceremony, soldiers of the *Ertuğrul* regiment marched in this area and sang, 'We are the soldiers of *Ertuğrul*, we are ready to die for the Sultan Abdülhamid' (2002, p. 42). With these words, past and present come together, supporting Abdülhamid's authority by that of *Ertuğrul* Bey. Furthermore, the architectural elements of *Ulu Cami*, the mosque that was built in the early days of the Ottomans, were used in the royal mosque in Abdülhamid's *Yıldız* Palace Complex. For example, every effort was extended to replicate the *minbar* of the *Ulu Cami* in the *Yıldız* Cami (2002, p. 40).

In addition this 'search for roots' has precedents in the 'roots' themselves. Deringil (2002, p. 42), indicates that Abdülhamid's 'obsession' with 'Ottoman roots' may be similar to Mehmet I's efforts to legitimize dynastic authority. Mehmet I had to struggle to hold onto power in the period of interregnum period that followed the Ottomans' defeat by Timur in Anatolia in 1402. As part of these efforts, he ordered the construction of a mosque in Söğüt, the first seat of the Ottomans. He was trying to draw connections to the birth of the Ottomans. Abdülhamid II attempted a similar task.

Sultan Abdülhamid II was trying to legitimize his authority and power, not only by referring to the distant past and the early days of Ottoman Empire, but also by glorifying the recent past. Fausto Zonaro's (1854–1929) reproduction of Bellini's (1429–1507) famous portrait of Mehmed II, which is now in Topkapı Palace Museum (Renda 1992, p. 462), can be interpreted as one example of that effort in the visual arts. In reproducing the portrait of Mehmed II, who is considered one of the most 'powerful' and 'greatest' sultans, who 'conquered' Istanbul, a 'glorious' and 'celebrated' history would be illustrated. A reproduction of Mahmud II's (1785–1839) portrait of Sclesinger, in which the Sultan is dressed in Western style, was made by French painter Bertaux (1843–1928) (Renda 1992, p. 461). Although the sultan was dressed in Western clothes in the original portrait, he is seen in traditional clothes in Bertaux's portrait. Mahmud II was the sultan who had made many social and military reforms and is generally considered a modern/Western sultan. Because Sultan Abdülhamid II was a modern monarch who formulated new education, health and industrial systems, while also promoting traditional values, this 'modern' sultan's traditional appearance in this portrait fits very well with the characteristics of the Hamidian era. Furthermore, Renda (1992, p. 462) claims that the sultan wanted to exhibit the portraits of those older sultans within the *Yıldız* Palace. The exact location of this planned display is unknown; however, in the section of Mozafar al-Din Shah's travel diary that describes his days in *Yıldız* Palace during his visit to Istanbul in 1900, (Mozafar al-Din Shah, 1903, p. 225), the shah discusses an underground gallery from *Şale* Kioks to the *Yıldız* theatre building, in which many portraits of older members of the Ottoman family and paintings of war scenes were hanging.

The glorification of the past was also achieved through the portraits of older Ottoman sultans applied on porcelain plates that were products of the *Yıldız Çini Fabrika-i Hümayun* (Imperial Yıldız Ceramic Factory), which was founded during the reign of Sultan Abdülhamid II. Ottoman sultans were depicted with the monumental buildings that were built under their patronage (Kürkman 2004, p. 178). On the first plate, we see a portrait of Sultan Abdülmecid and the *Dolmabahçe* Palace; on the second, Sultan Selim III and the barracks of *Selimiye;* and on the third Sultan Mahmud II and *Nusretiye* Mosque. While these depictions emphasize both the sultans' and their buildings' power, they also reinforce the power of Abdülhamid II, who was the patron of the production. In other words, they glorify the past in order to underline the power of Abdülhamid's regime. One could assume that, by sponsoring the production of those plates in the factory within his *Yıldız* Palace, Sultan Abdülhamid re-legitimized his dynastic power through his predecessors Abdülmecid, Mahmud II and Selim III, who were considered modernizing figures. From this point of view, with the products of a new,

Western and modern factory, Abdülhamid II was creating continuity with older Ottoman sultans in terms of their modernization efforts.

The Ottoman method of legitimizing authority was different from that of the Qajars. The Ottomans were interested in the early Ottoman era, aiming to highlight their dynastic power, while the Qajars attempted to create a dynastic lineage from ancient Iran through the Safavids. Abdülhamid II, like other Ottoman sultans, used his ancestors' power and authority to re-legitimize his own. While the 'obsession' with the Ottomans' roots can be identified as a way of going into the past in order to be purified, the obsession with the golden age was an effort to re-gain a splendour that had been lost by propagating a celebrated history. From this perspective, the Ottoman interest in history can be considered as a result of a 'break' with the past. The past was represented as nostalgia for a history that had already passed. However, the Qajar search for roots was neither purification nor nostalgia. It was related to the legitimization of authority. The Qajar dynasty's return to the ancient and Safavid past was an effort to present itself as the last part of this dynastic and cultural lineage. In other words, the Ottomans were searching for dynastic continuity; the Qajars were seeking dynastic legitimization.

The Western-modern dimension also shaped the Ottoman and Qajar political and social agenda of the nineteenth century. Active relations with Europe and modernization activities in education, the military, health and many other services constitute that Western dimension. Both states were engaged in modernization activities in order to be part of the 'modern' world. In the Ottoman Empire, construction of railway and telegraph services and the formation of school for girls were significant reforms in terms of modernization. Nasser al-Din Shah was reluctant to build the school for girls, unlike his counterpart Abdülhamid II; but he ordered construction of railway and telegraph service (Amanat 1998, p. 428). Discussing the modernization activities undertaken by these two states is beyond the scope of this paper, but my aim is to give a general idea about this process and introduce photography as a new, modern tool that performed a function long assigned to painting in terms of representing the past and modernity. In his article 'Powerful art of Qajar photography', Ali Behdad (2001, p. 149) states that 'photography displaced painting in creating "'an image of dynastic power" since the time of Nasser al-Din Shah'. He defines the photographs of Nasser al-Din Shah, taken himself with the assistance of Ghulam Huseyn Khan, that were given to *rijal* and local chieftains as 'tokens of his dynastic power' (*ibid* 2001, p. 149). Moving from this argument, we could say that photography displaced[4] painting not only in creating 'an image of dynastic power' but also in creating a new, traditional/historical and modern/Western nineteenth-century image in both Qajar Iran and the Ottoman Empire.

The 'Rise' of photography

The invention of photography presented a new tool for modernity. It belongs to Daguerre, who first invented the silver-coated copper plate prints in 1839. This new medium was 'discovered' and used by Ottomans and Iranians soon after its invention. Photography was introduced to the Empire by the Western traveller photographers who passed through Ottoman lands. Two Italian brothers, Carlo and Giovanni Naya, were the pioneers who established the first daguerreotype studios in Istanbul (Öztuncay 2003, p. 41) in 1845. The first studios were established during the reign of Sultan Abdülmecid (1839–1861), who, like his successor Sultan Abdülaziz (1861–1876), sponsored pioneers of photography. By the beginning of 1850 other photography studios, such as the Kargoupolos', were established and the daguerreotype became widespread in Istanbul (Öztuncay 2000, pp. 21–22).

In the early days of photography many traveller and local photographers were in Istanbul. Ferrier, Robertson, Abdullah *Frères*, Kargoupolos, Sebah and Joilier were the famous photographers who were photographing monuments and panoramic views as well as ordinary and royal people in those early days of photography in Istanbul, the 1860s and 1870s (Öztuncay 2003, p. 67). With the support of the Grand Vizier Keçecizade Fuad Paşa, Abdullah *Frères* had prepared a series of portraits of the members of the sultan's cabinet and after that, in 1863, they became court photographers during the reign of Sultan Abdulaziz (2003, p. 185).

4 'Displacement' does not implicate a shift in which painting was completely abandoned. It only emphasizes the power of the new medium of photography.

Although photography was introduced to the Ottoman Empire before Sultan Abdülhamid II's reign, it had its 'golden age' during reign, under his patronage. There were *fotografhanes* in *Mekteb-i Harbiyye*, *Mühendishane-i Berr-i Hümayun*, *Erkan-ı Harbiyye-i Umumiyye* (the General Staff) and *Matba'a-i Bahriyye* (the Naval Printing Office) by the end of the 1890s (Kaygusuz 2009, p. 81). The Sultan had a personal interest in photography, and a *fotografhane* was constructed within the *Yıldız Palace Complex* under his order (2009, p. 81). He gathered photographers under his patronage and sponsored them either by salary or prestige. Because they craved both material benefits and fame, one of the ultimate achievements for a photographer was to become a court photographer and to be honoured by the sultan with medals. It was difficult to earn that kind of fame and popularity, but it was easy to lose it. For example, Abdullah *Frères* lost the prestige that they had earned during the first years of the reign of Sultan Abdülhamid II when they photographed the Russian generals and ambassadors during the Russo-Ottoman War. Their place was later claimed by the photographer Kargaopaulos. A similar prestige would be earned by Sebah and Joailer even later (Özendes 1998, p. 83).

As was the case in the Ottoman Empire, Western and traveller photographers were the pioneers of photography in Iran. Jules Richard (1816–1891), a master of the daguerreotype, was one of first photographers in Iran. He came to Iran in 1844 and was appointed to the faculty of *Darolfonoon* in 1851 (Vuurman and Matens 1999, p. 20). Luigi Pesce, a master of the calotype process, came to Iran in 1848 and made many photographs of Tehran and Persepolis (*ibid* 1999, p. 20) Furthermore, an Italian missionary, Luigi Montabone, was entrusted with the task of making photographs of Iran. He travelled to Iran in 1862, and sixty-two albumen prints of his journey have been preserved (*ibid* 1999, p. 21).

Photography became widespread during the reign of Nasser al-Din Shah, who had a personal interest in the medium. Nasser al-Din Shah himself was an enthusiastic photographer and encouraged his courtiers to take up the art. A department was devoted to photography in *Darolfonoon*. Furthermore, as did his counterpart Sultan Abdülhamid II, the shah converted a building within the Golestan Palace into his *akskhana*. He took many photographs of the Golestan Palace, his courtiers and his women in addition to self-portraits.[5] Numerous photography studios were founded during the reign of Nasser al-Din Shah; photographers like Abdullah Qajar (1849–1850) and Antoine Sevruguin (1870–1930) built great reputations.

What were the reasons for the rapid rise of photography in both polities? What was the motivation for the rulers' patronage? The most important motive behind the rapid rise of photography was the rulers' hunger for information. Because photography was an effective way of being informed, many albums of landscapes, buildings and portraits were created from various regions within their lands and brought to both Sultan Abdülhamid II and Nasser al-Din Shah. There are numerous photographs from various corners of the country, taken on the orders of Sultan Abdülhamid II, in *Yıldız* Palace albums; photographs taken by order of Nasser al-Din Shah were kept in the Golestan Palace (Afshar 2002, p. 199). As Sultan Abdülhamid II rarely left his *Yıldız* Palace Complex – probably because of his fear of being assassinated – those photographs and albums played a crucial role in informing the sultan about his country. The sultan ordered many photographs of new, modern buildings, military services, organizations, museums and historical sites. Furthermore, photographs of technological developments, ceremonies and ancient sites were also sent to Nasser al-Din Shah. He himself asked photographers to take photographs of the ancient monuments of Iran, such as Persepolis (Vuurman and Matens 1999, p. 20).

Photographs were used not only as sources of information but also as gifts, part of the states' self-representation projects. Photography was linked with modernity while it also was used to represent heritage and emphasize cultural and political power. Albums including portraits as well as images of new buildings, factories, schools and hospitals, namely the 'modern' face, together with the ancient and historical sites of the Ottoman Empire and Qajar Iran were sent to various rulers and royal family members. A document shows Prince Bismark's appreciation for Sultan Abdülhamid II after the latter had sent some photographs to the Prince.[6] In another document the German king and queen thank Şehzade Burhaneddin and Naile

5 Golestan Palace Archives album no: 894/447 includes photographs taken by Nasser al-Din Shah himself.

6 BOA Y.PRK.EŞA 7/5.

Sultan for the photographs that they had sent.[7] Certain photographic albums, which were known as 'Hamidian Albums', were sent as gifts to the Library of Congress in 1893 and the British Museum in 1894 (Gavin 1989). These gifts exhibitied the 'modern' and 'Western' Ottoman Empire while underlining its historical heritage. Moreover, there are some albums sent to Iran during the reign of Sultan Abdülhamid II that are now in Golestan Palace Archives. One of those albums includes selections of historical and touristic sites of Istanbul together with panaromas and everyday scenes.[8] Another album, including photographs of his visit to Istanbul, was given to Mozafar al-Din Shah (1853–1907) while he was in Istanbul.[9] This album also includes photos of Ottoman factories such as *Yıldız Çini Fabrika-i Hümayun*, museums and scenes from historical places such as Palestine, mosques of Bursa and Beykoz kiosk of İstanbul. In other words, in addition to serving as a 'memory' of the shah's days in İstanbul, this album also represents both the historical and modern faces of the Ottoman Empire.

Furthermore, the Iranian monarchs, especially Nasser al-Din Shah and Mozafar al-Din Shah, sent albums abroad as gifts. A document from the Ottoman State Archives indicates that two such albums were sent to the Ottoman Empire, although we do not know exactly where they are now.[10]

Furthermore, there are two albums sent from Iran to the Ottoman ruler or elites in the Taksim Atatürk Library.[11] One album comprises portraits and photographs of people from particular trades, mostly by Sevruguin; the other presents a selection of landscapes, buildings, people from various trades and costumes. On the back cover of those albums 'A. Tarnawski, Relieur de S.M.I. le Sultan' is written (fig. 2). This inscription indicates that the covers were made by the royal bookbinder Tarnawski, whose name is seen on many covers of Hamidian albums. Due to the presence of the name of the royal bookbinder, we might consider these albums royal gifts presented to the sultan; however, they include photographs of eroticized

---

7 BOA Y.PRK.EŞA 10/87.

8 Golestan Palace Archives, album no 491.

9 'Albüm Takdimi', 3 October 1900, *İkdam*, p. 1. Golestan Palace Archives, album no 389.

10 BOA Y, AZJ. 30/52.

11 These albums are in Taksim Atatürk Library Rare Collection. Album no: 63–64.

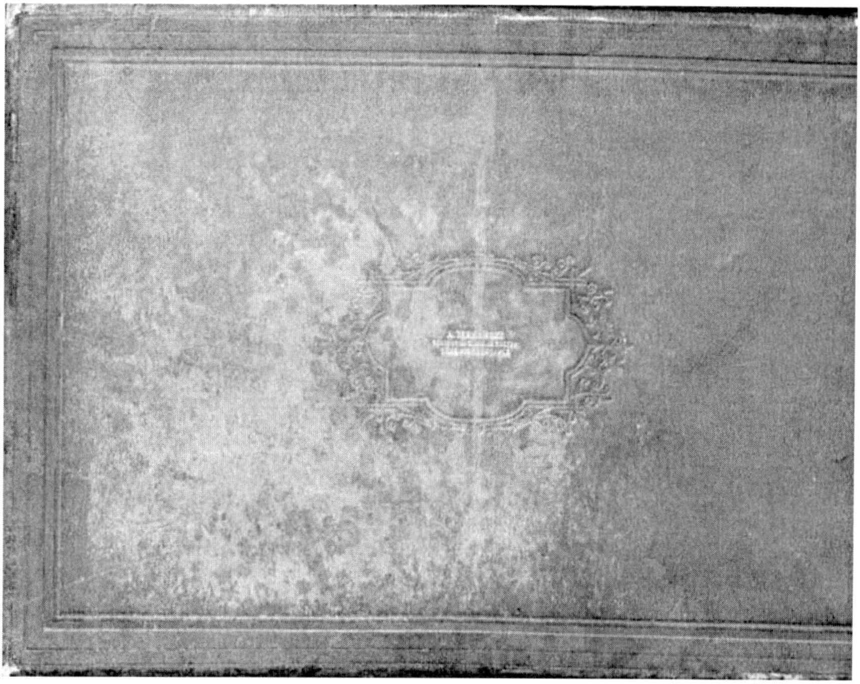

Figure 2

women, which brings doubt to this theory. Because Sultan Abdülhamid II was a religious person and there was a strict censorship on many sexual issues (together with political, economic and social issues) during his reign, I am reluctant to assume that these albums were royal gifts sent by the Iranian ruler to the Ottoman sultan. Furthermore, the order of the photographs in the albums supports this doubt. These albums include two photographs of Mozafar al-Din Shah at a young age (fig. 3), which suggests that the ruler during that period was Nasser al-Din Shah. However, Nasser al-Din Shah is not the main figure, as would be expected in a royal album sent to another ruler. There is no portrait of the Nasser al-Din Shah; he appears only in one photograph, at a dinner, surrounded by other people (fig. 4). All of these characteristics bring two possibilities to mind: photographs, including two portraits of himself, were selected and sent by Mirza Mozafar al-Din to an Ottoman prince or official, or these two albums represent Qajar photographs collected by an Ottoman elite. Whether they were royal gifts or not, they reveal that Qajar photographs were circulating within the Ottoman Empire and were collected or covered by the royal bookbinder.

Photographic portraiture

The invention of photography expanded portraiture in terms of its accessibility and reproducibility. As the camera became more accessible and photography studios more numerous, being photographed became a regular activity. Among the photographs taken in the Ottoman Empire, the highlights are the portraits of the sultan, princes, men, women and children from the dynastic family, *paşa*s, ambassadors from various countries as well as foreign generals and their wives and children. Additionally, there are portraits of *Mevlevi Şeyh*s, Christian and Jewish ecclesiastics, the photographers themselves and their families. Photographs that represent different occupations and ethnicities, such as beggars and gypsies, are also extant. On the other hand, in Qajar Iran we see photographs of the shah, his high officials, *ulama* (religious scholars), people from various professions, eroticized women and the royal harem (who were personally photographed by Nasser al-Din Shah himself).

i) Royal portraiture

As photography became a regular practice, many photographs of the rulers and dynastic families were made. We could easily say that royal photographic portraiture followed the painting tradition in terms of creating continuity with the past and propagating dynastic power. In Qajar Iran, traditional themes and concepts were used within the royal portraiture practice, through which continuity with the past was achieved. As an example, emphasis on the ancient and traditional elements of Iran is observed through some photographs of Nasser al-Din Shah. The shah is seen as an authoritative and powerful figure in many of those portrait photographs. He is sometimes sitting on a chair, carrying medals and aigrette and holding a sword. One portrait photograph in which he is seen in front of the *Peacock*

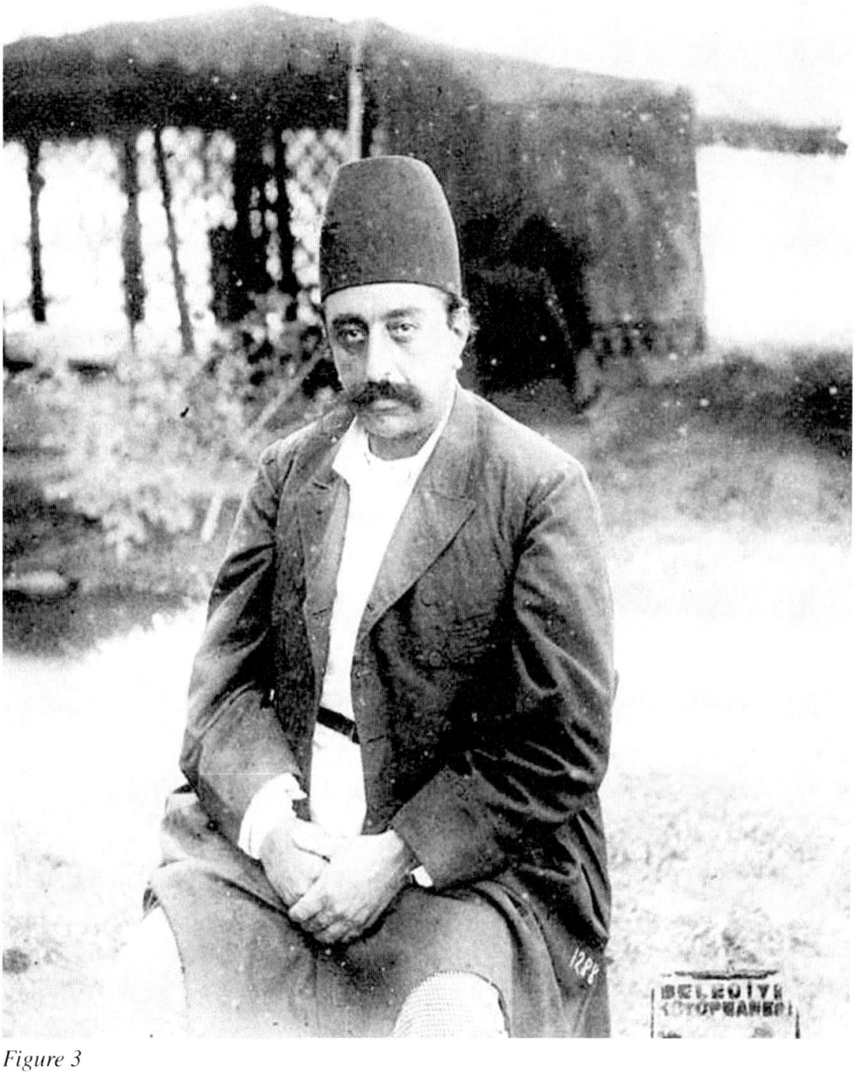

Figure 3

Throne (fig. 3) not only demonstrates 'his monarchial power and his dynastic affiliation with Nadir Shah Afshar' (Behdad 2001, p. 149) but also reminds the viewer of traditional royal painted portraits, such as *Muraqqaʿ* and *Shahanshahnama*. That is, it represents monarchical power by showing the ruler on the royal throne, which is considered a sign of royal power and authority.

Traditional hunting imagery is also seen in photograph form. In some photographs, Nasser al-Din Shah is seen in hunting scenes as a victorious huntsman sitting behind an animal (fig. 4). These hunting scenes are reminiscent of ancient rock reliefs from Iran's Achemenid (550–331 B.C) and Sasanian (A.D. 221–642) past as well as the rock reliefs of Qajar ruler Fath ʿAli Shah, which were sited strategically in relation to the former (Diba 1998, p. 32). The reliefs that Fath ʿAli Shah added to the ancient examples in *Taq-i Bustan* are the most famous. Moreover, there are eight additional reliefs: seven from Fath ʿAli Shah's and one from Nasser al-Din Shah's reign (Luft 2001, p. 32). Rock reliefs on the banks of the Savashi River north of the village of Jalisjand, in the district of Firuzkuh, depict a huge hunting scene with Fath ʿAli Shah in the centre, surrounded by twenty-one of his sons and courtiers (*ibid* 2001, p. 32). Moreover, in the reliefs in Ray the ruler is represented as a lion hunter. Hunting photographs of Nasser al-Din Shah are likely intended to draw connections with ancient Iran and recall such rock reliefs. Nasser al-Din Shah continued the tradition of hunting imagery by using a new method: photography. We can assume that photography contributed to the use of ancient vocabulary; it displaced painting and carving in the portrayal of hunting scenes.

While Nasser al-Din Shah was using photography and his portraits in order to demonstrate his authority and create a dynastic image, Sultan Abdülhamid II was using the 'non-existence' of his portraits for the same purpose. Although Sultan Abdülhamid II supported the activity of making the old Ottoman sultans' portraits, he was reluctant to pose for his own portrait. Abdullah *Frères*, who had already made photographic copies of older Ottoman sultans' painted portraits (Eldem 2004, p. 29), were punished by the sultan once for taking his photograph and copying his portrait photograph

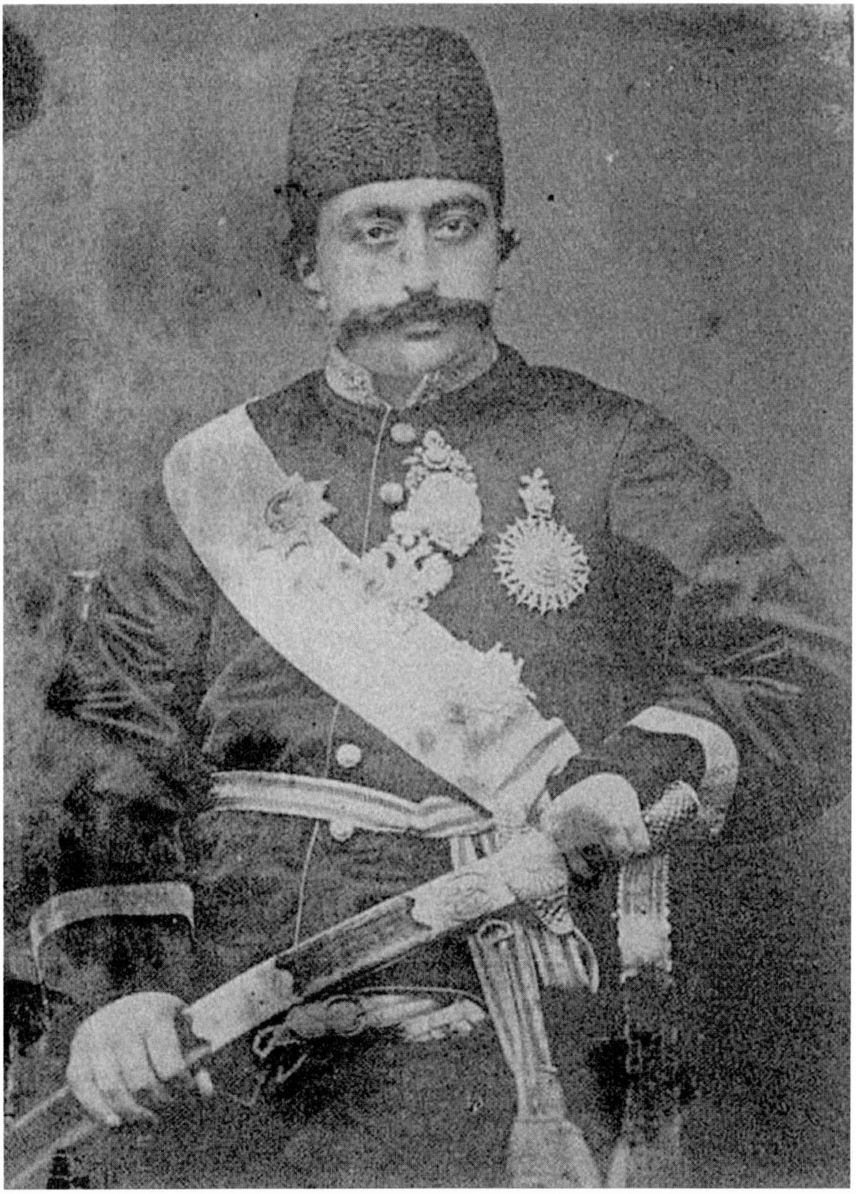

Figure 4

without his permission.[12] While the sultan wanted to use the images of the older sultans in order to create connections with a powerful past, he did not want his own image to be seen. During Abdülhamid's reign, anyone could write an informative letter, named with the French word *jurnal*, directly to the sultan. Often, these letters did nor provide any kind of information, but were a form of spying. In other words, people wrote about what others were doing and even took money from the courts in return. The ear of the sultan was everywhere, via his spies and surveillance; he did not need to be visible. He had the power of invisibility; his image on display could harm that kind of power. However, this does not mean that the sultan was never photographed; it only emphasizes his reluctance to pose.

Portraiture: representing modernity

It was not a coincidence that the first photography education was established in the schools of *Darolfonon*; photography was understood as a new science, which would capture 'reality'. Underneath a Qajar photograph in which some men are standing in front of a wall talking to each other while others are gambling (Semsar 2003, p. 461), it is written that 'these people were photographed in their natural posture' (*halat-i tabiyye*). Using the word '*halat-i tabiyye*', the photographer (or someone else who wrote it) intended to declare that he captured reality. Furthermore, in the Persian newspaper *Nasıri* an article mentions that after the discovery of the camera, a new tool that makes photographs of a dream was invented.[13] It was announced as making photographs of what people had in their minds. In addition to 'capturing the real', this machine would make shots of the 'unreal'. This article manifests the expectations of photography as a new, modern technology.

This modern technology itself played a role in capturing 'modernity'. In addition to the photographs of modern buildings, new educational, health and military services, police organizations, factories and the railway, modernity was also represented through portraiture. Some objects – such as camera itself, which was a 'modern' and 'Western' instrument

[12] BOA. Y.PRK.BŞK. 4/33.

[13] *Nasıri*, 20 September 1896, no: 20, p. 7.

in the nineteenth-century Middle East, chairs, tables, clocks and the like that we can consider Western objects – are seen in many portraits. One could assume that through these objects manifestation of modernity was achieved. Furthermore, Vuurman and Matens (1999, p. 26) mention that after Sevruguin gave him two photographs of a ballet dancer, Nasser al-Din Shah began to use a *tutu* in the photographs of his harem that he himself took. In addition to aesthetic desires, the *tutu* with which many Qajar royal harem women pose was probably used because of its Western affiliation. Furthermore, a portrait in which a Qajar harem woman is seen with a piano (Semsar 2003, p. 160), which was a 'Western' instrument, also had an affiliation with modernity. Although there were many photographs that depicted women as objects of 'exotic desire', such as the photograph of a half-naked woman lying on the floor, posing with a pipe (fig. 4), those photographs of women with Western objects are significant in terms of representing modernity. In addition to the 'oriental imagery', this 'modern imagery' also appears in many photographs.

Furthermore, both in the Ottoman Empire and in Qajar Iran criminals who were brought to police stations (Öztuncay 2005, p. 29) or held in prisons were photographed for the record.[14] Photography was also used in the investigation of the attempted bomb assassination of Sultan Abdülhamid II, and photographs of the people responsible for the act were published.[15] Gendarmerie Minister Kamil Paşa was assigned the duty of founding a photography workshop within the ministry building, and the court photographer Vasilakis Kargapoulos was entrusted with the workshop (Öztuncay 2000, p. 72). Similarly, in Qajar Iran many photographs of prisoners were taken.[16] Perhaps these photographs were taken for official records, in order to identify the prisoners and guards, but they also functioned as part of the state's control mechanism for informing the shah. Although they were official records, they also represented the justice, order, control and power of both states. They became tools for representing both of these polities as modern states able to take control of criminals in modern prisons. By pho-

[14] BOA DH.MKT 2023/71; BOA BEO, 101, 7549.

[15] BOA Y.E.E 1082. Also see: Öztuncay 2005: p. 29.

[16] For example, a photograph of a prisoner is in Golestan Palace Archives, no: 347/32.

tographing modernity, both states were capturing and manifesting the state as a part of the modern, Western world.

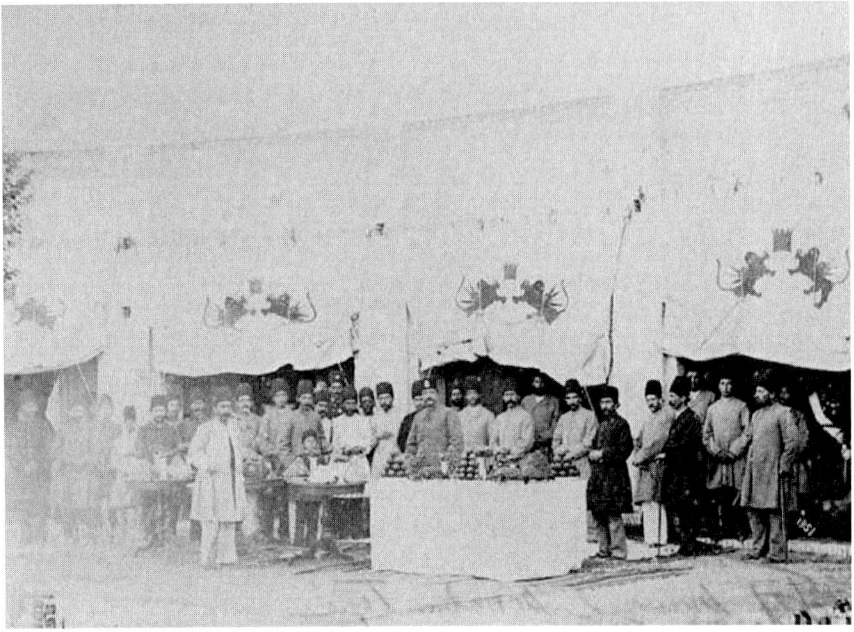

Figure 5

An album dated 1881 comprises ninety photographs of high officials of Yıldız Palace during the reign of Sultan Abdülhamid II.[17] Every page includes four portraits, and the series begin with the title '*Yaveran-ı Hazret-i Padişahiyan Kulları*' (*aid de-camp* subjects of his excellency) (fig. 5) and the two subtitles '*Yaveran Kulları*' (*aid de-camp* subjects) (fig. 6) and '*Çavuşan Kulları*'(sergeant subjects) (fig. 7). The album has a thick red cover which has the sultan's *tuğra* on it (fig. 8).

In the photographs all of the *yaveran* and *çavuşan* are standing in front of similar backdrops and generally looking directly into the camera with same looks and gestures. This 'ordered' characteristic of the album makes the subjects recognizable while also representing an echo of the 'orderly'

[17] Taksim Atatürk Library Rare Collection, Alb 0063.

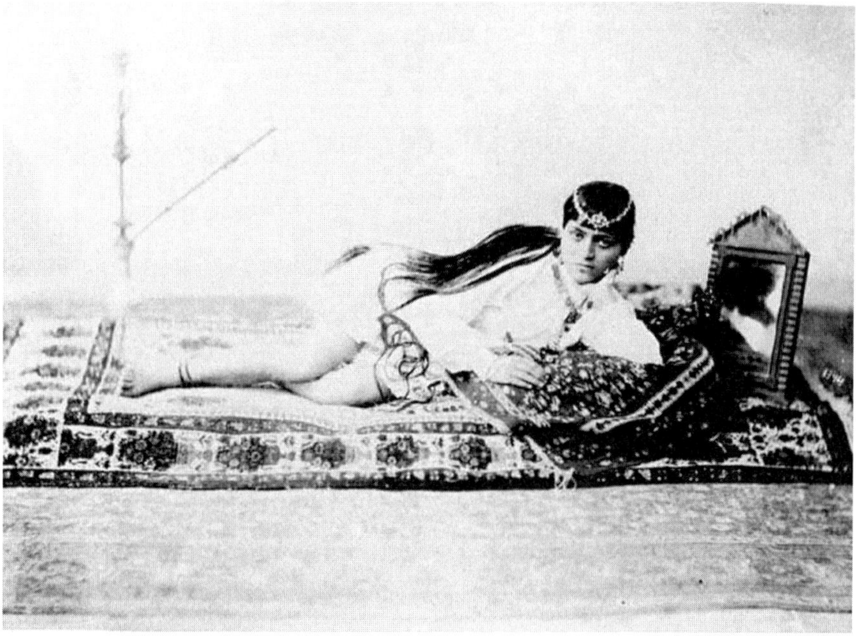

Figure 6

Hamidian state. This album fits very well with the attempt to create a modern state image in terms of presenting a visual document of Western-dressed officers depicted as orderly.

ii) Pride and privilege[18]

The album of *Yaveran-ı Hazret-i Padişahiyan Kulları* must have been prepared by the order of the sultan, or at least with his permission. As a visual record, the album can be considered a result of the sultan's desire to be informed about the subjects within his palace; however, it goes beyond this function. This album attributes privilege to those who were photographed. First, to be selected for an album made for the sultan was an honour; second, the artistic composition of the photographs emphasizes the privilege of the subjects. *paşas* pose in a studio in front of a backdrop, dressed in uniforms

[18] This is the title of Edhem Eldem's book *Pride and Privilege* 2004.

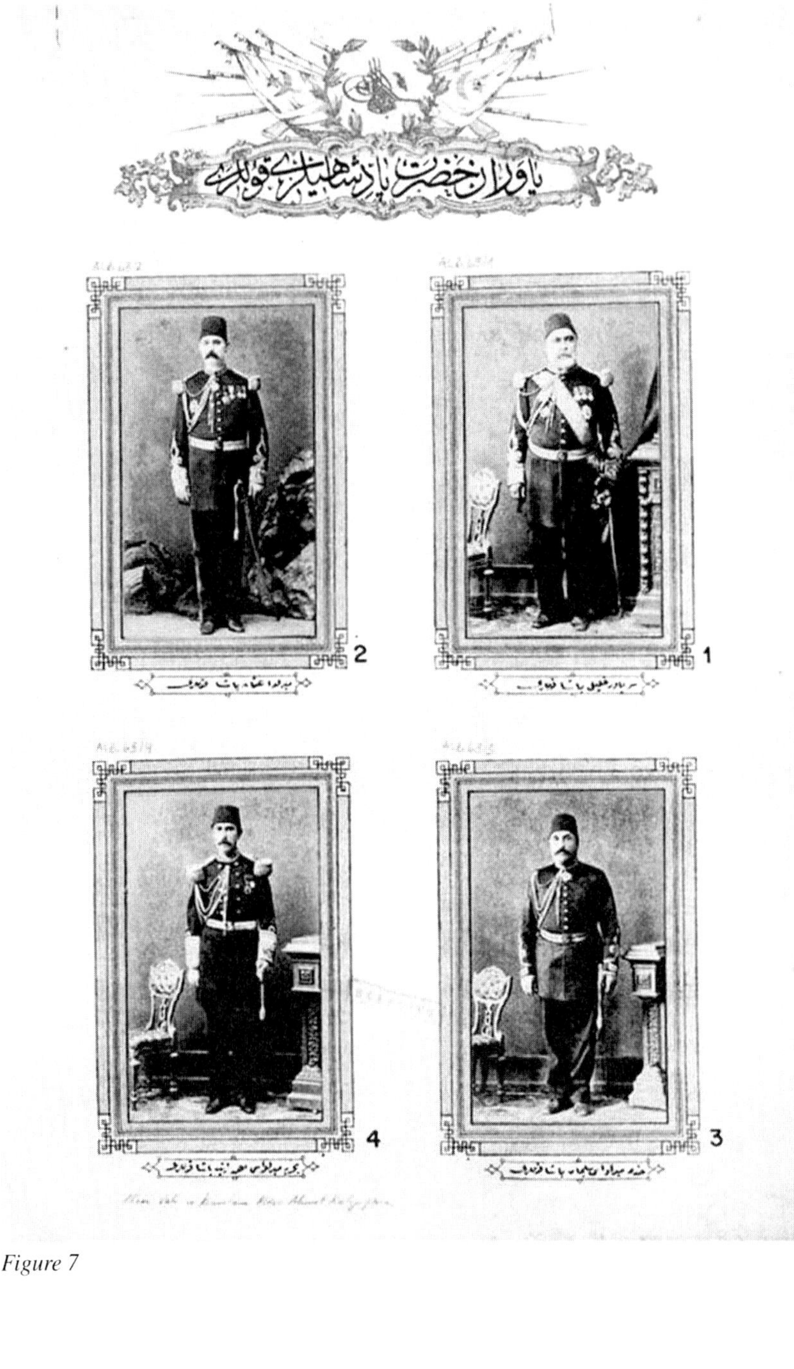

Figure 7

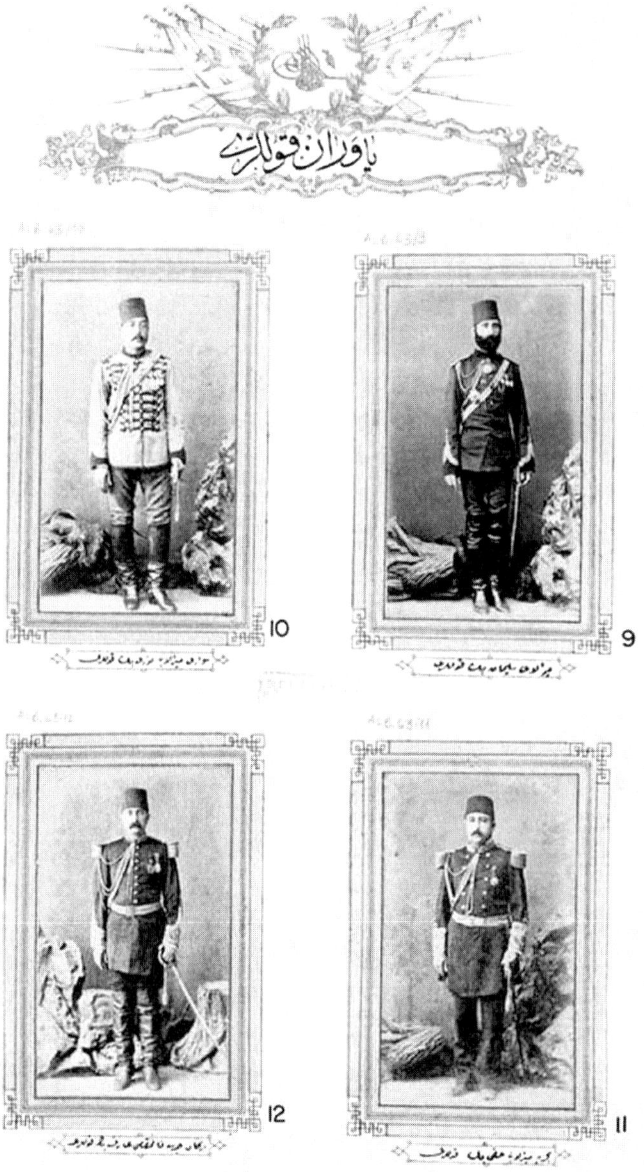

Figure 8

and carrying their medals, which were significant signs of being privileged. While *yaveran* (*aid de-camps*) hold their swords, *çavuşan* (sergeants) carry their guns.

The artistic set-up that is achieved through the accessories – including apparel, medals, badges, headgear, swords and other features such as the person's look and standing posture – that are noticed in many portrait photographs. The subject who was photographed was represented in a position according to his or her social status. Medals and badges were among the most significant accessories reflecting a person's social status and privilege. Sultan Abdülhamid II, Nasser al-Din and Mozafar al-Din Shah honoured many *paşa*s, bureaucrats and foreign officials with massive numbers of badges. So many badges were granted in Abdülhamid's reign that the situation, which was heavily criticized, became material for caricaturists and satirists. The caricature that Said Paşa couldn't handle the weight of his medals and collapsed is a good example of those reactions (Eldem 2004, p. 335). Jakob Landou states that the great number of badges granted during Sultan Abdülhamid II's reign caused a decline in their value (cited in Eldem 2004, p. 333). According to Selim Deringil, Landou is 'wrong' in his argument. Deringil believes instead that those badges were symbols of 'involvement in the system' and that their purpose was to arouse good faith in the minds of the acceptors (cited in Eldem 2004, p. 333). Edhem Eldem states that both opinions are acceptable as they reflect the characteristic of Abdülhamid's reign. Because modernism and conservatism do not exclude each other, positive use and abuse of medals reflect that characteristic of Abdülhamid's reign (*ibid* 2004, p. 333). Moving on from Deringil's 'symbol of involvement' definition, we can consider these portraits manifestations of being involved in the system.

Photography had a rapid ascension for practical reasons and replaced painting in creating the 'dynastic image' that has been mentioned in this essay; it is also very interesting that photography – especially portrait photography – came into fashion in both states. With the development of studio photography, portrait photographs became widespread. Walking into a studio and having one's photograph taken was something only a person of significant economic power could do. Thus, many *paşa*s, bureaucrats, merchants and their wives and children became regular visitors to those studios. The two portraits of the Ottoman *Serhafiye* (chief surveillant) Ahmed Celaleddin Paşa, taken twenty years after the former one (*ibid* 2004, pp. 340–41), displays the increase in the number of his medals and badges. Medals are the focus of the latter example, while the former presents an image of an Ottoman paşa with modern dress, holding his sword. We can observe a similar change in two subsequent photographs of Gazi Osman Paşa (*ibid* 2004, pp. 338–9). While one of his early portraits shows him as an Ottoman paşa with two medals, standing and holding his sword, the second portrait, which was taken twenty years after the first, displays his excessive number of medals. As the number of medals and badges increases, the portraits focus on them to a greater degree, probably as a result of the *paşas*' and photographers' desires. Additionally, the desire to be photographed with an increasing number of medals can be interpreted as a rivalry among the privileged. Taking into consideration that these portraits were taken in well-known studios by well-known photographers, it is highly possible that the *paşas* were well aware of each other's portraits. Their eagerness to be photographed with constantly increasing numbers of medals and badges can be interpreted as an expression of that rivalry. Those portraits of people who were photographed together with their accessories, especially medals, first represented their social class, power, pride and privilege, and then represented the power of the rulers, the shah and the sultan who gave them that privilege.

Moreover, as Eldem states, Sultan Abdülhamid II decided to create a medal for women, following European examples. Because women did not have much chance to have *Osmani* and *Mecidi* medals in a world that privileged men, a special medal named *Şefkat* was created for them (*ibid* 2004, p. 260). As an example, the *Şefkat* medal was given to Fatma Aliye, a famous Ottoman intellectual, due to her contributions in collecting money for the poor.[19] Additionally, a medal named *Afitab* was designed for the women of the royal family as well as foreign queens and princess in Qajar Iran in 1873, shortly before the Ottoman invention of *Şefkat* (2004, p. 260). The portraits of privileged women who were given that medal by the sultan express not only the privilege of the women who carry it by its braid but also

[19] Taksim Atatürk Library Rare Collection, FA_EVR_000021-026.

the power and 'merciful' nature of the sultan, who created a special medal for them.

In addition to these, in Qajar Iran there are many photographs of *ulama* (scholars of religion). This is probably related to the relationship between the shah and the *ulama* as well as *ulama's* attitude toward the visual arts. Although Nasser al-Din Shah was not much loved by the *ulama* – as was his ancestor Fath ʿAli Shah, who was regarded as a *Na'ib Khass* special deputy) of the *Sahib al-Zaman* (lord of the age: the hidden imam) (Hambly 1968–91, p. 161) – he had a balanced relationship with the *ulama*. In addition, *ulama* supported the visual arts in Qajar Iran. By extension of Diba's argument that the 'images were deemed acceptable when they utilized the vocabulary of ancient Iran or were located in court context' (Diba 1998, p. 44), we can add that they supported Nasser al-Din Shah's efforts to use visual art due to its relation with Shiism as well, as we see in *taʿzieh*. In other words, the *ulama* supported visual arts if they presented continuity with the ancient and Islamic past. Taking the *ulama*'s support for visual arts into consideration, it is not strange that they did not oppose the use of photography and even posed for the camera[20] (fig. 9).

On the other hand, it is not possible to find many photographs of the *ulama* in the Ottoman Empire although there are portraits of *Mevlevi Şeyh*s as well as Christian and Jewish ecclesiastics. In the Ottoman Empire the *ulama* did not act against the visual arts, including photography, but we nevertheless cannot say that they supported artistic activities. So, the non-existence of photographs of the *ulama* for public use must be related to the relations between the sultan and the *ulama*. There was an uneasy relationship between the sultan and *ulama*; indeed, *Şeyhülislam* as the head of the *ulama* had accepted Sultan Abdülaziz's *dethronement*, which ended in a murder or suicide. Additionally, Abdülhamid II was a reformist sultan who formulated modern systems while using the ideals of Islamism. He was personally a religious person but his Islamism was limited to symbols, titles and charities. The sultan never let the *ulama* become too powerful, thinking that they likely would not accept his modernist reforms, especially those in the educational system, such as the establishment of school for girls.

[20] For example, there is a photograph of *ulema* in Golestan Palace archives no: 1415/11.

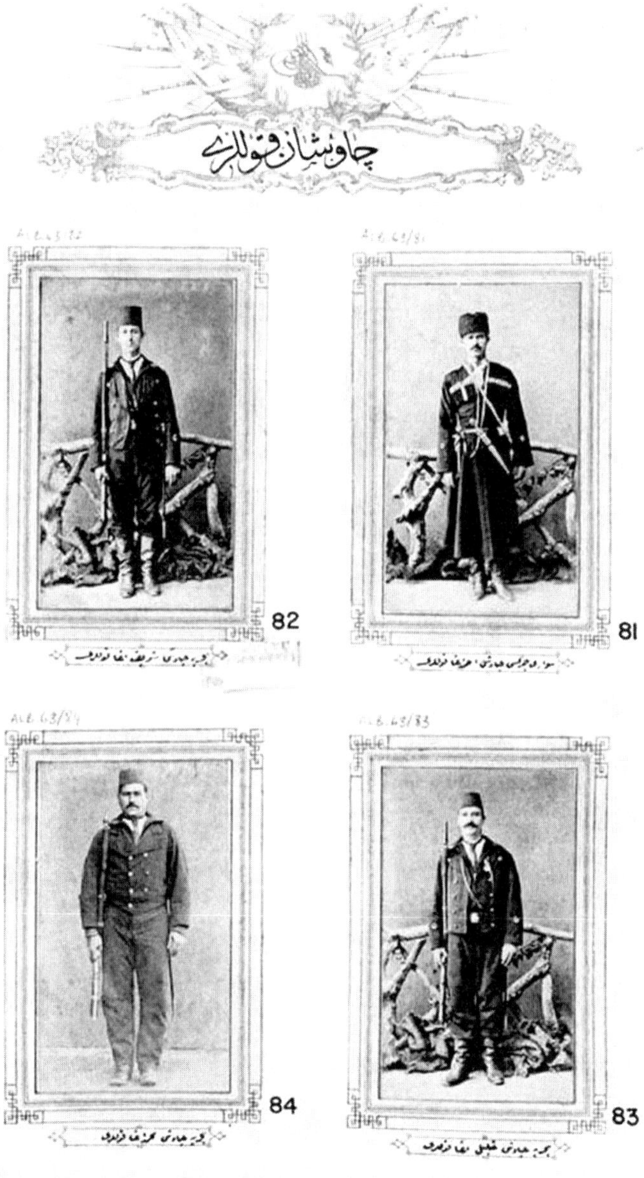

Figure 9

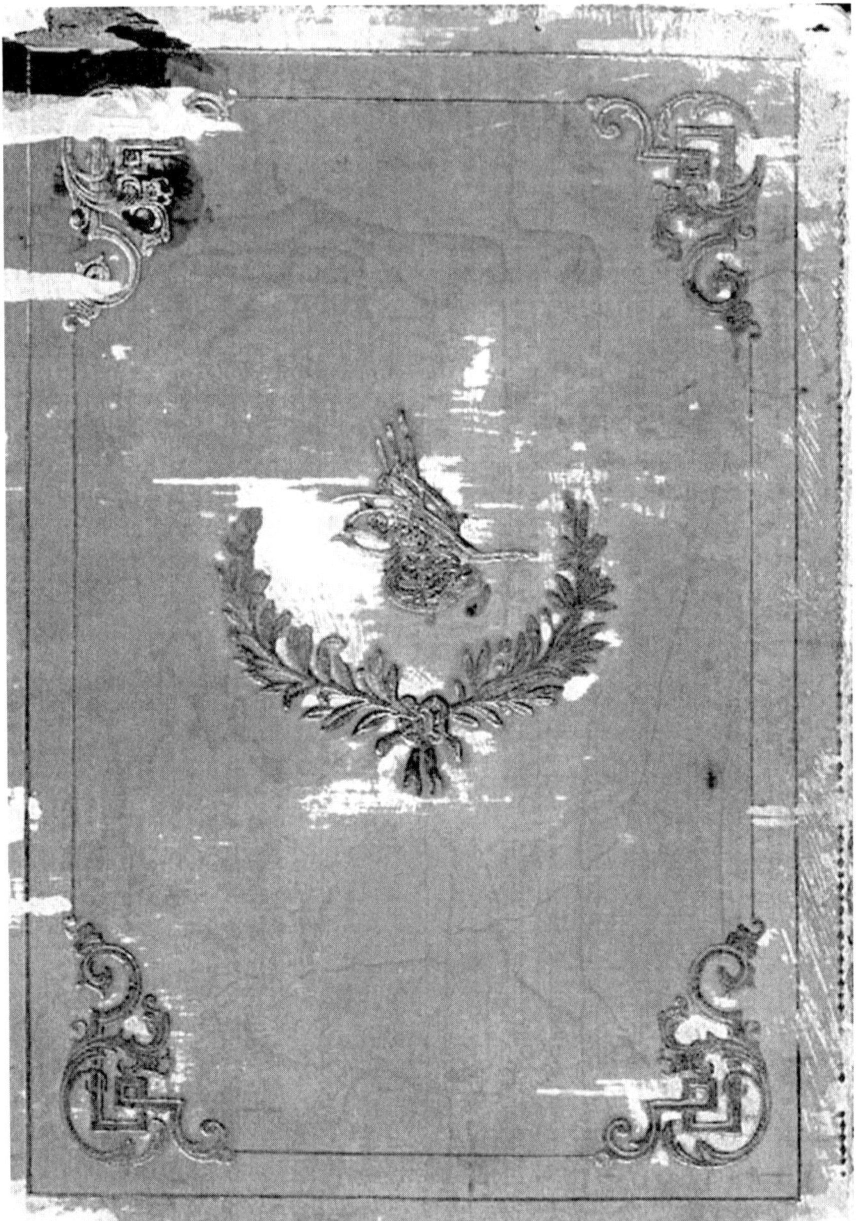

Figure 10

However, the aforementioned matters do not explain whether the *ulama* had photographs for private use. There is a photograph of *Şeyhülislam* Cemaleddin Efendi (Demirel 2007, p. 101), but we do not know when and under which conditions the photograph was taken or how it was used. One could assume that the *ulama* were reluctant to be photographed because of the debate regarding human imagery in Islam. On the other hand, because the *ulama* did not act against visual arts, including photography, this assumption does not explain the entire situation.

Concluding remarks

This chapter explored the use of portraiture in nineteenth-century Iran and the Ottoman Empire with a comparative approach. In addition to the ways in which portraiture was used to reinforce official authority and create continuity with the past in order to propagate dynastic power, this paper also examined the influence of modern notions on the portraiture tradition of the two geographical and cultural neighbours. While undertaking discussions on methodology and making thematic comparisons, I also tried to touch upon the relations between the two states – although this topic is not the primary motivation behind the writing of this paper. In order to understand the visual arts in both states in the nineteenth century, one must examine political and cultural relations of the two states. Examining the Ottoman-Qajar cultural and artistic environment from a comparative perspective and analysing the political, social and cultural relations between these states will bring additional insights into the mentality of that era.

Tracking a modern visual element through two similar conditions of chaos

From the post-revolution era in France to the post-constitutional revolution days in Iran

Siamak Hajimohammad

Introduction

As one opens Karl Marx's *Eighteenth Brumaire of Louis Bonaparte*, one reads the following in the first paragraph of the first chapter: 'Hegel says somewhere that great historic facts and personages recur twice. He forgot to add: Once as tragedy, and again as farce' (Marx 1999, p. 1).

Although the translator has remarked in the Persian translation that Hegel never expressed such an idea, the truth of the statement is emphasized here regardless of whether it was spoken by Hegel or Marx during their debates and discussions with Engels (Marx 1999, p. 10). The difference, however, lies in the fact that this chapter has applied the idea to the field of visual arts while adding the following two notes to it: significant historical facts recur frequently, not only twice, in similar ways, and what happens after the first event is not a historical farce but, in many cases, very significant tragedies.

The story of Colonel Muhammad Taqi Khan Pessiyan (1892–1921) and his severed head is among such events. Accordingly, this presentation assumes that the comparison of Iran during the time of Reza Khan's rise to power and Napoleonic France – despite the very short range of Iran's social movements – is more or less applicable, given the similarities between the socio-political events of the two eras and especially their cultural and artistic outputs. In other words, although there were absolutely no tangible relations between Iranian photographers and nineteenth-century French artists, certain images have been created under similar circumstances during these eras of turmoil, and such images depict specific social situations with their basic differences and similarities. Such situations could only be expressed linguistically as the establishment of a modern structure in society.

Picture of the Colonel's head

The first time the author encountered the picture of Colonel Muhammad Taqi Khan's severed head – among many other memorable pictures in Muʿayirulmulk's album in the Manuscripts section of the University of Tehran's Central Library – he was overcome by an air of unfamiliarity. There was no information about this picture, which appeared somewhat remarkable as it depicted a severed head and yet was found among a large number of family photos of the political figures contemporary with Muʿayir.

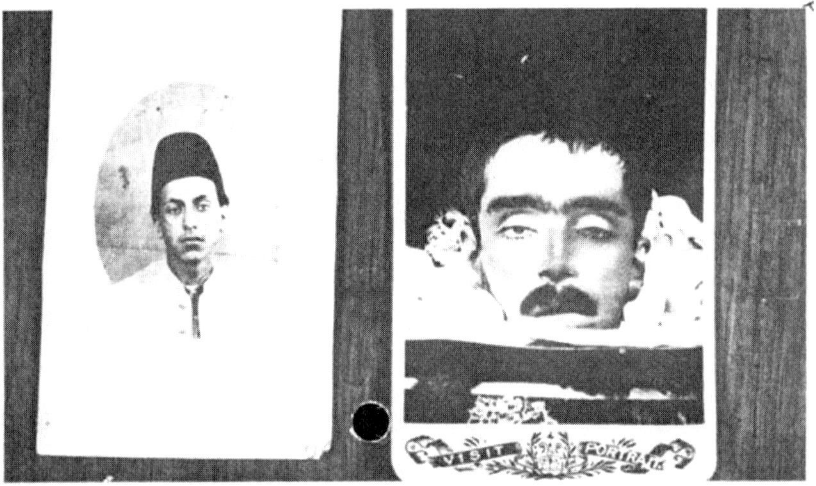

Figure 1: Exhibit 56 in Muʿayir's collection (the Manuscripts Section of the University of Tehran's Central Library)

The stillness seen in this anonymous face, among so many well-known figures, was an undoubtedly unique sight. The logo of the anonymous atelier under the picture somehow led one to draw the conclusion that the collection's owner had likely added this photo to his album of many renowned figures merely for amusement.

Further investigation confirmed that the face was actually far from anonymous and, indeed, a most eminent figure of his age. It is almost universally the case that wherever one searches Colonel Pessiyan, he or she finds a copy of this picture. Ironically, as this picture has not been specified anywhere under the Colonel's name and was not published in any official Iranian newspaper along with the news of his death, it is only the recurrence of the photo in the various references that compels us to ascribe it to him.

Most references state that there are two versions of this picture, forming the following two arguments. One is the non-manipulated version above: a photo that might be considered the 'raw picture' taken by the Quchani photographer. In this photo, which resembles a simple portrait, the head has been put directly in front of the camera, surrounded by white textile to hide the neck injuries (fig. 2). Some say that there exists a visit card of the Colonel's head because of its representation type in similar photo collections of the University of Tehran. The author, however, could not find such a card.[1]

The other image is a version decorated with a poem by ʿArif Qazvini (1882–1934), likely made to be used as a postcard (Sheikh 2007). This picture (fig. 3) has its roots in the aforesaid raw picture; however, it undoubtedly was prepared after the Colonel's funeral, as it is said that Qazvini composed this poem offhand on the funeral day (Azari 1974).

The renowned poet's lines seem to be attached to the picture as a measure to honour the name of the Colonel – a national hero – so that the public could be provided with such a picture. A part of the people's visual perception of the history of the Constitutional Revolution (and its subsequent occurrences) is realized via the release of such pictures in the form of postcards (Sheikh 2007).

The Colonel's head is known as such in most references, and this generality lies in the visual perception accompanied by Qazvini's poetry, thereby

[1] Obviously, with respect to the subject in question, there was no need to search such a visit card.

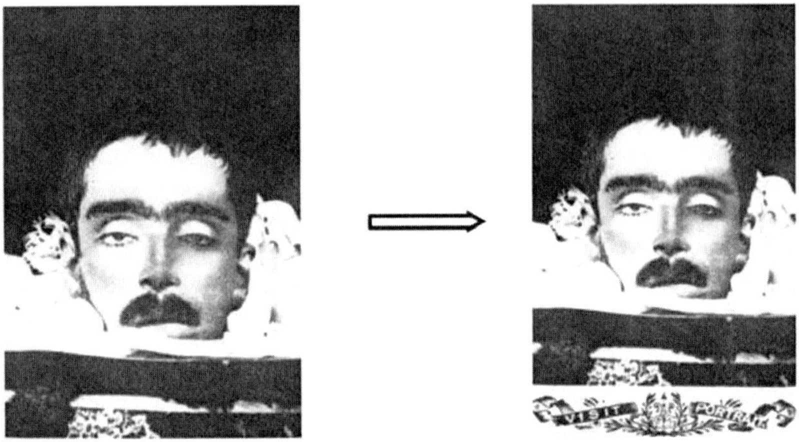

Figure 2: Raw Picture

prompting the audience to unite with the concept of nationality rather than any other notion and to develop an epic impression of the character of this impassive face.

Both pictures originate from the same negative; they have been cropped differently, but the source of both is the original photo taken of the Colonel's head on the day after his death and promised by the Kurd commanders to be sent to Tehran.

In summary, both versions have one feature in common as far as the current study is concerned: the picture of Colonel Pessiyan, whether a national hero or an outlaw, whose blank face in the picture archived in the personal album of a politically high-ranking family would be indicative of a victory. This image is tied to the sociopolitical process of the conceptualization of the newborn Iranian national identity.

Sociopolitical circumstances in the last years of the Qajar reign

As Ahmad Shah sat on the throne of Iran during World War I, the country's declaration of neutrality was practically ignored by the states involved. Severe conflicts between the two major parliamentary parties, the Democrats and the Moderates, lingered as the third parliament was inaugurating, and,

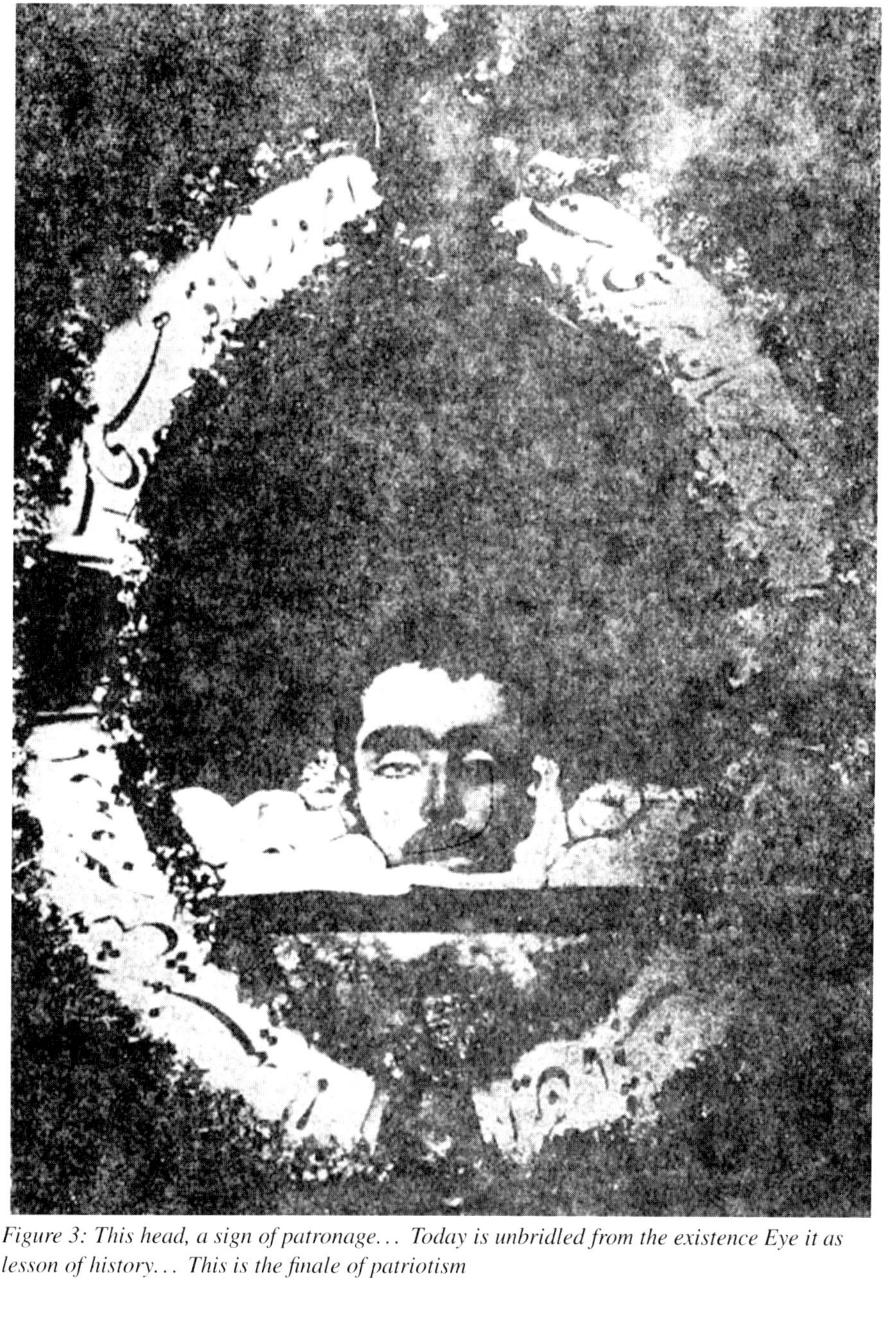

Figure 3: This head, a sign of patronage… Today is unbridled from the existence Eye it as lesson of history… This is the finale of patriotism

on the streets, bloody confrontations occurred between their armed advocates. The democrats' typically extremist socialist mottos placed them opposite the constant support of the moderates for feudal grandees and the traditional middle class. Nevertheless, national unity, a regular army, and an inclusive independent tax system were emphasized in the plans of both parties (Abrahamian 2000).

The first serious upheavals against the foreign presence targeted the British forces in the south of Iran. Tsarist Russia occupied the Caspian Sea's southern states and issued an ultimatum to Tehran. This was followed by the resignation of Mostowfi ol-Mamalek's government (in office 1910–1911) and the dissolution of the parliament. Britain formed the South Persia Rifle (1916) in the south of Iran to face turbulent immigrant tribes. Iran desperately acknowledged the 1915 Treaty with Russia, according to which the state was divided into two parts: one ruled by the Russian authority and the other governed by the British forces. In 1917 the Bolshevik Revolution broke out throughout the Russian Empire and the Russian forces left Iran. Consequently, Britain took control of some entities, including the Cossack Forces, that were previously governed by Russia. Britain attempted to fill Russia's absence in the occupied lands. In 1917 the cabinet of the 1919 Treaty was formed by Vosugh od-Dowlih (1868–1950). The central government was involved in some clashes with the rebels in Isfahan and Kashan (Katouzian 2008).

Comprehending the concept of nationality as a modern term[2] was an outcome of the courses of action that were triggered a century before the notion reached Iran, in such countries as France, whose people are among the pioneers of the concepts of constitutional governments and social revolutions.

The engenderment of the concept of Iranian nationality in its modern form was realized as an undeniable outcome of a revolution decorated with the title 'Constitutional'. However, because a long period of chaos (1906–

---

[2] The notions of modern, modernity and modernism appear in this text as defined by Cyrus Yeganeh in his *Modernization and Post-Modernization* 2007. 'Modernity' refers to all dimensions of modern life, while modernism explicitly aims at modern art. Accordingly, the term *modern* is used where it is possible to address the least associations of modernity.

25) occurred in Iran immediately after the formation of the first parliament, this newborn nationality continuously underwent inevitable changes. The under-formation of the Iranian identity suffered one of its absolute damages in World War I, when the states at war ignored Iran's independence.

The next serious damage occurred with the 1919 Treaty conclusion. Britain, who was now at the end of a significant war, saw the field evacuated by its old rival, Russia, and could not become involved in Iran's affairs, as it did in the pre-war years. On the other hand, it neither intended to repeat nor was capable of repeating its Indian experience (direct intervention) in Iran. At the same time, the danger of the new Bolsheviks threatened the entire region. To escape the predicament, Britain had no option but to help a mighty central government rise to power in Iran; this government would, as much as possible, be harmonized with British interests in addition to serving as a barrier against the imminent danger of Bolshevism in India (Abrahamian 2000).

While the primary purpose in the rather long-term plan was realized with Reza Khan's rise to power, the secondary aim, as a short-term plan, was accomplished in the terms of the 1919 Treaty. Nevertheless, as addressed before, the reinforcement of national identity was inevitably the overarching goal shared by both plans.

As matter of fact, contrary to the very humiliating appearance of the 1919 Treaty for Iran, there were different debates regarding respect for Iranians' national identity. World War I was the first difficult battle delineating the concept of a gap between nations. Under such circumstances, in addition to its own interests, Britain was desperate to recognize Iranian national identity. According to the documents of the 1919 Treaty, the British side frequently emphasized concern about encountering the wave of nationalism (Katouzian 2007).

The 1919 Treaty was concluded as the most prominent opprobrium of all time to confront inland oppositions. After the War, the Russians stepped into Iran in the form of the Red Army, but this time they were in support of the Forest Movement led by Mirza Kuchak Khan. The Khiabani Movement was also formed in 1920 in Tabriz.

Vosugh od-Dowlih fell and Moshir od-Dolih (in office 1871–1873) rose to power (when Colonel Muhammad Taqi Khan was sent on a mission to

Khorasan). The men of Tangistan were suppressed. The Forest Movement suffered a divide, and Khiyabani was repressed and executed by the Cossack forces in Tabriz. Moshirodoleh resigned afterward, to be replaced by Fathullah Khan Akbar (1855–1938), the senior commander of Gilan (Katouzian 2008).

After a long time there appeared a symbol of centralized power: the coup d'état (21 February 1919) was staged with the introduction of two prominent figures. Siyid Zia Tabatabayi (1888–1069) started the revocation of the 1919 Treaty so that an image of dignity could be formed in the public mindset, and trust in the administration was boosted as a result of the establishment of the national army by Reza Khan.

The joint Reza Khan-Seyed Zia administration signed an amity accord with the Soviet Union, as a result of which the latter ceased its support for the Forest Movement. This agreement added to the internal problems and further led to Reza Khan's victory and the repression of the Forest Movement.

Next, Reza Khan's rise to power adopted a twofold nature for men of thought: on the one hand, he took action to repress internal riots, such as those of Shikh Khazʿal, to unify Iran, form a consolidated army, etc., and became a national symbol in the imperious renovation pattern (Tavakoli 2008); on the other hand, these actions resulted in serious confrontations with the most loyal forces to the cause of Constitutionalism, in such a way that they were killed or degenerated into rebels and public enemies.

However, the half-ruined structure of Siyid Zia's administration was internally shaken again. Reza Khan's endeavour led to the replacement of Siyid Zia with Qavam ol-Saltanih (1876–1955), who also advocated progression. Reza Khan, the icon of modern nationalism, gained more momentum on a daily basis and won reign over all of the country following a four-year campaign. He attained this glory by forming a regular army, repressing oppositions, revoking the 1919 Treaty, establishing a bureaucratic structure and commencing fundamental constructions.

This paper has thus far described the process through which the newborn structure of national Iranian identity was built. This lean and feeble structure was, however, ill-fated, as it disintegrated in a flood of incidents, ultimately being laid in a bed where it could be described as having relative stability in terms of a symbol named Reza Khan. The following section discusses the realization of this concept in the picture that is the focus of this paper, in comparison with a similar picture produced twenty years after the French Revolution.

Theodore Géricault: A Short History

In Géricault's painting, the man's sunken eyes, overflowing with death and terror, meet our own. Turning back to the Colonel's visage, what one sees in his eyes is very different. Géricault intensifies the violence of such a death by means of traces of dried blood on the subject's white background, while the Quchani photographer covers his own prudency before a man renowned for liberality in a white textile by covering his sinews.

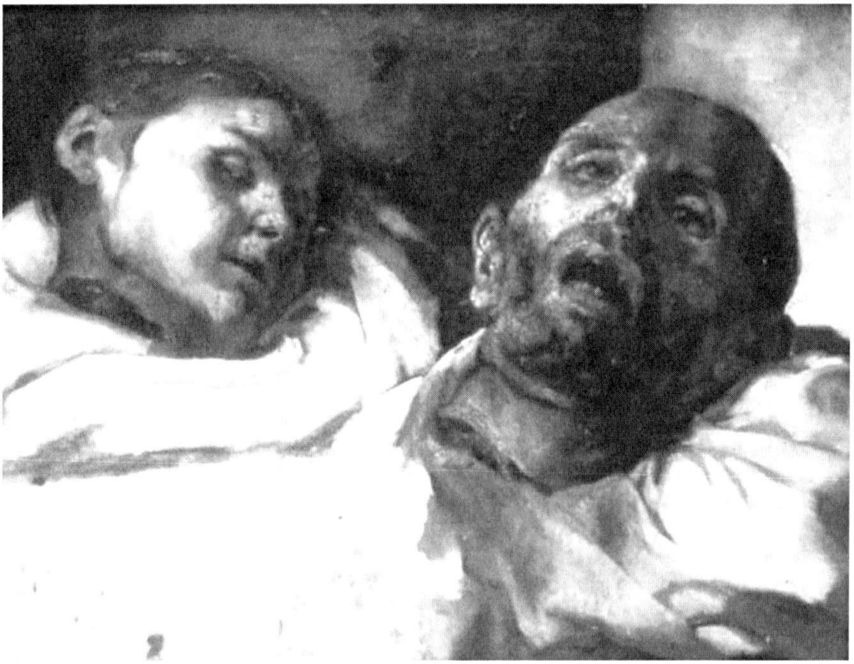

Figure 4: Theodore Géricault, Severed Heads, 1818

What inspired the author to write this chapter was the apparent similarity between the picture of the Colonel's head and the above painting.

The traces of dried blood on the textile in the background and its link to a bodiless head lead us to visualize a horrendous scene. Considering the year in which the painting was made, the inevitable interpretation seems to be that it depicts the results of guillotine executions or the reign of terror that lasted, uninterrupted, from the late eighteenth century to the mid nineteenth century. The sociopolitical circumstances of Iran described above suggest the similarity of conditions in which the images were produced.

In 1789, the French Revolution was won with the conquest of Bastille, and the old feudalism was replaced by the new French bourgeoisie in the political cycle. Riots and opposition against modern France immediately spread throughout Europe. The European empires, whose rules were supported by the pillars of Christianity and feudal structures, rapidly rose against this new framework of the French Republic in the form of the First Coalition in 1792.

The French nobles who had escaped to Italy and England almost immediately began their counterrevolutionary activities. Under these circumstances, revolutionary forces were scattered because of internal and external pressures. The First Reign of Terror began in 1793; in only seven weeks 1,376 men and women were guillotined (Durant & Durant 2008). In 1794, the First Reign of Terror seemingly reached its end through the guillotining of the Robespierre brothers. However, the story was to be continued.

Napoleon (like Reza Khan) rose as a simple military officer from his hometown on Corsica (an island in southwest Italy) and gradually seized power[3]. However, when Napoleon ended *The Directory*[4] on the eighteenth of Brumaire, 1799, he indeed put an end to an era of riot and launched a period of national unity and the establishment of a unified France. During his empire, Napoleon actualized national French identity yet brought about a turbulent era of war and anxiety inside central France. By challenging

---

3 Here the purpose is by no means to deem the movements of Reza Shah's age the same as those of Napoleon, as the author understands that these two eras are not comparable in terms of scope, organization, details and depth of movements. Nevertheless, the two events can be compared in terms of general similarities such as main titles, general events and roles of individuals

4 A five-handed board of French Republic Administrative Department from November 2, 1795, to November 9, 1799 (the 18th Brumaire of 1799).

feudal Europe, he waged a battle with the bourgeoisie and feudal lords. The core of modern nations appeared from the heart of this battle (while Napoleon took action in regard to inland repression and made most of the primary arms of the revolution disappear). By laying siege to Brie[5] and enslaving all of the inhabitants of his occupied territories in Europe – by levying heavy taxes and compelling them to pay the costs of his great army – Napoleon more or less eliminated the growing bourgeoisie and reigning lords of these countries in favour of the growing French industrial bourgeoisie (Tarle 2008).

In 1814, the Third Coalition started its final battle with Napoleon, and in 1815, Louis XVIII was enthroned as the French king. Despite of the significant changes that occurred in the financial and administrative systems as well as in the French army under the reign of Napoleon, constitutional monarchy was re-established and the title 'republic' was removed. Upon the re-establishment of monarchy the old ruling system enacted a massive retaliation. The guillotine, which was removed as a revolutionary symbol, was returned to the administrative justice cycle.

Théodore Géricault produced his most significant works between 1814 and 1824, amidst a hurricane that swung France between the two poles of a monarchy and a republic/empire that had created an image of national identity. *The Raft of the Medusa*[6] is perhaps Géricault's most important work; the artist is thought to have spent much time in hospitals and dissection rooms where the dead bodies and limbs of executed people were kept. He then took the severed pieces of these bodies to his workshop so that he could prepare sketches for *The Raft of the Medusa*. However, Athanassoglou argues that works that have been understood as a sketches were not preliminary sketches for *Medusa* but also most of them had been depicted as a perfect painting while they were never exhibited for years after the artist's death. Nevertheless, Géricault's frequent presence in such places signifies the structural relationship between his works and his interest in medical sciences and human anatomy (Athanassoglou-Kallmyer 1992).

When Géricault died only three of his works were known, and they

5 A city in Belgium where the economic siege of Napoleon against England was signed.

6 As the picture is not structurally related to the text, it has not been included.

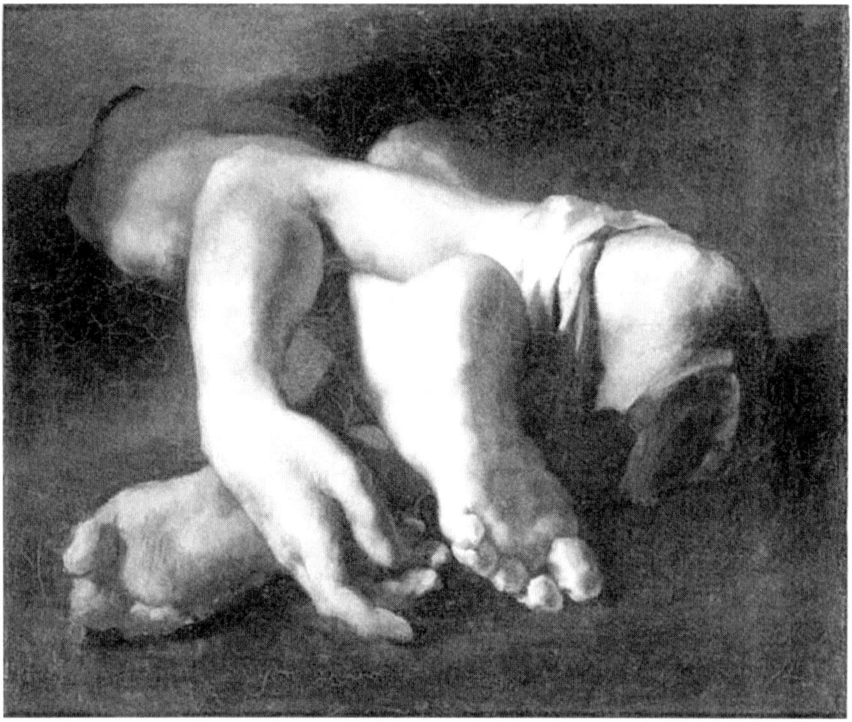

Figure 5: Théodore Géricault: Severed Limbs, 1818

remained Europe until the 1960s and 70s (Mishory 1997). The period in which Géricault's works were not publicly exhibited occurred at a time when his favourite works addressed different aspects in a way that Athanassoglou interprets them as showing interest in some sort of *fashion* (Athanassoglou-Kallmyer 1992).

In the early 1820s in France three or four people on average were executed each day. Because the executions were performed by means of guillotines and in large numbers, they prompted the French people to recall the *Terror* of the revolutionary era; they chose the title *White Terror* for that period of time (Athanassoglou-Kallmyer 1992). Terror in its social and political senses prevailed over Géricault's life and works. The violent representation of this turbulent era was effected by two basic approaches to the cultural atmosphere in which Géricault lived. In this era, some groups in European communities called for basic social reforms like revocation of the death sentence (or at least legalization of its process and removal of the guillotine). On the other hand, an extensive volume of literature and drama could be seen until 1830 whose main topic is a type of fantasy terror that deals with the fermentation of the real terror atmosphere, transforming it into a form that would be resisted and consumed by the public. This was indeed a pulp literature that produced many species of bloodthirsty creatures (e.g., Comte Dracula) under the title *genre noir*. It was of the same type described above as being fashionable: 'Géricault's paintings and drawings of the decapitated head treads the uncertain ground between empathetic social statement and delight in social horror (Athanassoglou-Kallmyer 1992, p. 610).

This structural duality in Géricault's works could be generalized to the valuation difference between high human morality and a certain type of moral perversion.[7] This interpretation of conceptual bipolar fluctuation in the intellectual atmosphere of Géricault's age, through an imperfect but efficient approximation, could be deemed true in regards to the atmosphere (production and consumption) surrounding the photo of Colonel Pessyan's head. There are also two fluctuation poles between some sort of moral growth and decline, a status which includes rather detailed definitions appropriate to Iran's specific circumstances, described in the following part of the paper.

Fragment as a metaphor of modernity[8]

Thus far, this chapter has presented a brief history of the sociopolitical circumstances in which the two pictures in question were produced. The author has attempted to link the three main concepts addressed in the paper: entry into modernity; chaotic eras which blend with movements toward modernity as a result of civil revolutions and subsequently change into an atmosphere dominant over the production of cultural outputs in the society; and, finally, the concept of *modern national identity*, which, in a structural

7 Athanassoglou, in part of her article, believes some human tendencies to be the reason of sexual perversions, necrophilia and sadism.

8 For more information in this regarad, see: Nochlin 2001.

relationship with these chaotic eras, was born as an introduction to modernity in different social circumstances.

Now a fourth main concept is added, which, at least, could be deemed the connecting point of many concepts with the prefix 'modern-', if not cast in the primary role. The fragmentation quality is a process of comprehending a phenomenon as a specific part against an inconceivable whole. Understanding this comprehension process would be further possible through a brief look at the methodology of natural sciences in the study of phenomena. For instance, one can consider medical sciences: the human body undergoes dissection as a medical research case (object), meaning that the body is fragmented into its components (cut into pieces) for rather close examination. In this case, a type of paradox appears: on the one hand, comprehension of the body as a whole is impossible without fragmentation (the inconceivable whole); on the other hand, a full comprehension of the whole human body could only be realized through its fragmentation process and the comprehension of each fragment as an independent phenomenon followed by the rearrangement of these fragments. Thus, the modern phenomenon cannot be separated from the *fragment* concept, as modern comprehension is only possible via *fragmentation*.

However, perhaps the major discussion in this paper, apart from the *fragmentation* process of a basic modern feature, is related to representation. In this regard, Linda Nochlin (2001) provides a useful statement. She has traced the *fragmentation* quality as a basic structure of modern portraiture from late eighteenth-century paintings to the photography of the late nineteenth century. She deems Géricault's works as having special significance, which provides us with the main connecting point to the entry of modernity into Iran.

Fragmentation as a common feature among many pictures of the French Revolution era sometimes occurs by direct representation of a fragmented part of the body and sometimes is depicted in terms of the general narration of a magnificent, entity-crushing story:

> The heart of this iconography of destruction, however, lies in that archetype of human dismemberment constituted by the guillotining of the victims of the Terror. The guillotine itself was figured as uniquely modern in the revolutionary imagination… in depersonalization the solemn occasion of public execution; in serializ-

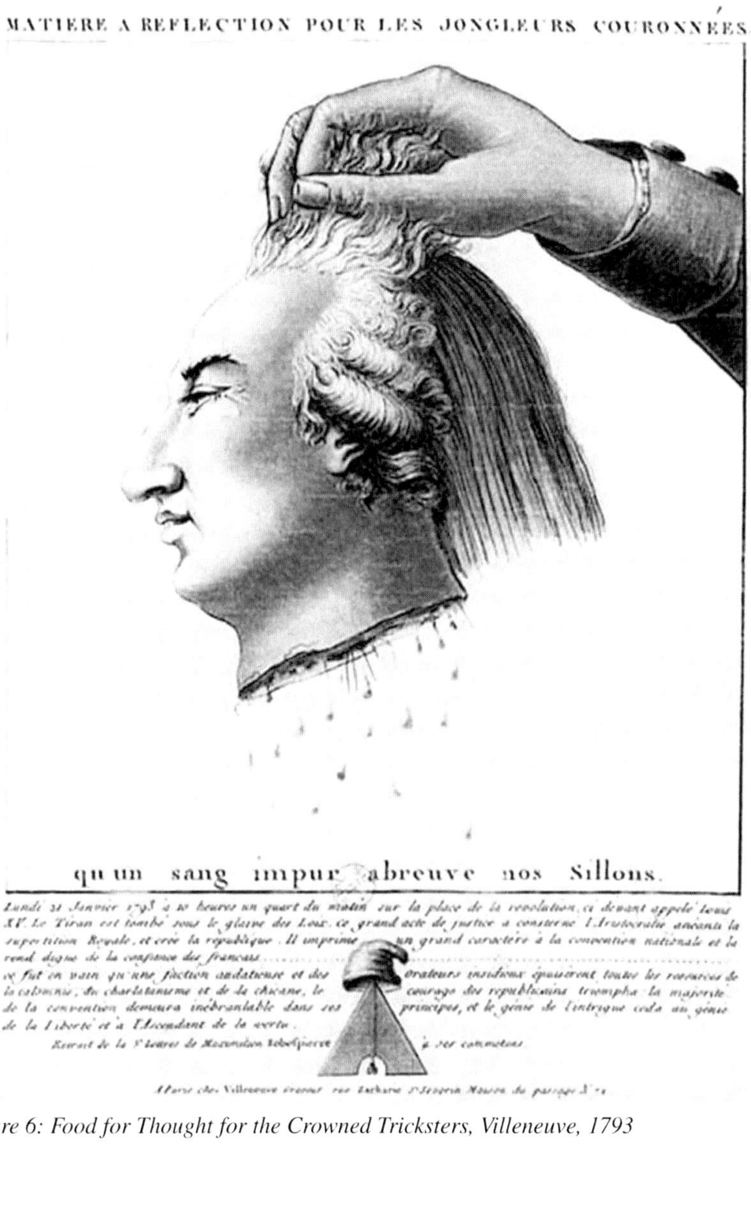

Figure 6: Food for Thought for the Crowned Tricksters, Villeneuve, 1793

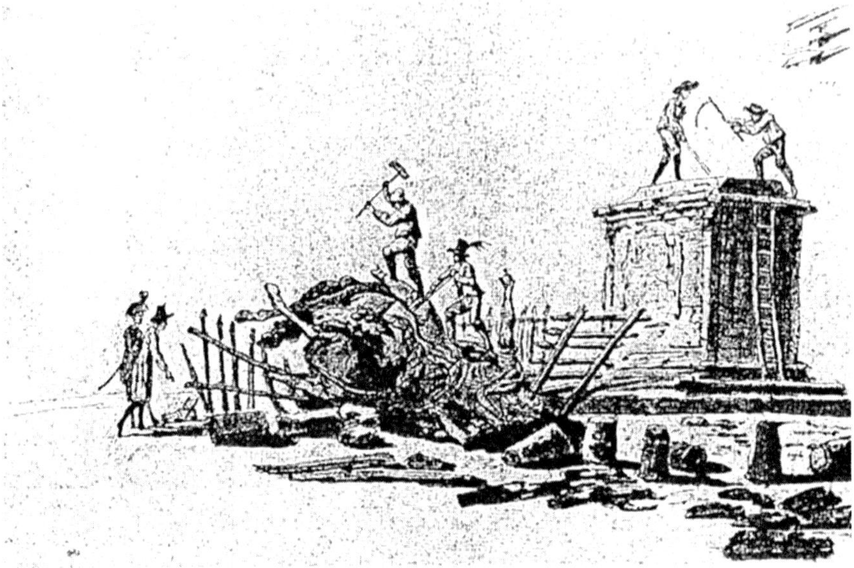

Figure 7: Destruction of the Equestrian Statue of Louis, Jacque Bertaux

ing and standardizing the act; in the supposedly scientific efficacy in its technology; and, above all, in its 'instantaneity', its reduction of temporal span associated with death to a mere blink of the eye, the guillotine was viewed as a specifically contemporary instrument of *state*/sanctioned death. (Nochlin 2001, p. 10)

Nochlin studies this *heart of iconography* in images with the subject of *king execution* as the old integrity symbol and, in a destruction and reconstruction process, puts us equal to the replacement of the old system busy with creating the new world. A paradoxical feature of this type of revolution representation and its associated chaos come to the fore:

Put in the simplest term, the omnipresence of the fragment – in variety of forms and with a wide range of possible significance – in the visual representation of the French Revolution had something to do with the fact that the French Revolution was caught in the throes of destroying a civilization before creating a new one. (Nochlin 2001, p. 10)

The author, through alignment of the *fragmentation* act with *sacrifice* and by linking it to the [no longer] sacred identity of the king, describes the excellence quality of dismemberment representation. Thus, in the custom of the revolutionary execution scene representation, the sacredness once possessed by the king is transferred to the revolutionary figure. Nochlin reminds us that we are facing a duality when we recall the revolutionary figure as the previously inferior man who has now occupied such a noble seat by means of a revolution: 'At the opposite pole of Revolutionary representation lies the topic of fragmentation as obscenity' (Nochlin 2001, p. 15).

Thus far, *fragmentation* is placed between two specific and semantically opposite points, which are only symbolized in a revolutionary situation: destruction/creation and inferiority/excellence. Thereafter, Nochlin, through her study of Géricault, points out that he is the one who 'most violently exploits the message castration implicit in the representation of the fragmented, or wounded male body' and links the artist to the heart of her historical study, which is 'the loss of French political potency after the fall of Napoleon' in addition to the attribution of the *mutilation* concept to such pictures. Here, Nochlin emphasizes that Géricault, in many of his paintings of injured men, depicted the *'Napoleonic antihero'* (Nochlin 2001, p. 16).

Nochlin, like Athanassoglou, stresses the strong visual relationship between Géricault's works and scientific objectivity or, in other words, 'the cool, clinical observation of the dissecting table' (Athanassoglou-Kallmyer,1992; Nochlin 2001, p. 18).

Finally, Nochlin believes Géricault's use of the horizontal frame to be a measure to emphasize 'romantic horror' in the picture as well as to point out the 'absolute abjectness of these subjects'. According to Nochlin, borrowing from Rosalind Krauss, this horizontal surface has a 'desublimatory' characteristic that first enables the comparison of such pictures with vertical frame pictures as 'the axis of beauty' and then brings them into the objects territory via putting the human head in 'the horizontal surface' (Nochlin 2001, pp. 20–21).

The representation of concepts relevant to the structure of a social change (a revolution and the consequent chaotic sociopolitical circumstances) in the form of *fragmentation* or dismemberment, as a modernity-associated element, encompasses all of the above-mentioned features of the transition period. *Fragment* is linked to the foundation of the modern world – i.e., science – because of its scientific structure. We welcome a new creation by crushing the past's magnificence into its fragments, creating our antihero and making him reach a peak of another type by putting an end to an old sacredness, stressing his earthly essence by representing him on an even surface, and challenging gods via this earthly characteristic. And, after all, we come to grieve his loss once we sacrifice him.

Concluding remarks

The political and social activists of the Constitutional Revolution fought for constitutional monarchy. Their ambitions were not practically realized. The balance of sociopolitical groups was disrupted, and, in the following years, the demands of the revolutionaries changed from constitutional monarchy to a republican government and from a democratic republic to an inevitable dictatorship. This chaotic replacement process led to some of the aforesaid movements.

The favourite topics in the political discourse of the time in Iran, particularly during Reza Shah's capture of power, included republican government, freedom, equality, authoritative central government, unity and emphasis on a single, unified Iranian nationality to achieve the primary symbols of modernity and progress, in contrast to the tribalism reigning over different parts of Iran (Abrahamian 2000). Such circumstances were established as a result of the universal atmosphere after World War I, as it was indeed this war in which *nationalities*, in their *modern* sense, confronted one another for the first time.

Such a status in Iran can be compared to the post-French Revolution conditions in terms of events such as the presence of some figures (i.e., Reza Khan and Napoleon), the pretext of political discourse (i.e., debates and discussions around unity, modernity, and central authoritative and precautionary measures to avoid the disintegration of the nation), and, finally, the terror due to the central government's encounter with divergent groups.

We return now to the two pictures that have been produced in two similar social circumstances and have similar visual features. The photo of the Colonel's head could be deemed an instance of a *fragment* form representation and the inevitable result of a transition era. The photo, more or less, shares the features and qualities attributed to pictures produced by Géricault and some of his contemporary figures. Obviously, this picture as described in the early nineteenth century is not a part of a stylistic movement but a merely inevitable event. Nevertheless, it is to be noted that, although cutting the Colonel's head off of his body and its representation in different forms somewhat appears to be an event, the release of these photos as outstanding examples of *fragment form* linked with science as the foundation of modernity (see the dissecting table) occurs exactly at a time that, according to what has been underscored by many scholars, is known as the starting point of the establishment of modern structures in Iran. Thus, the prelude of entry into modern Iran could be an event of this type.

It is important to remember that this image represents not only a photo but also a production and consumption process of such pictures[9]. Once the Quchani Kurds arrived in Quchan with the Colonel's head, they promised to send the photo to Qavam ol-saltaneh; therefore, the photo's first function in terms of a documented picture was known. Although the other versions of the photo in question have not been accessible to the author, the two versions addressed are indicative of the fact that at one time this photo, like those of Sattar Khan and Baqir Khan during the Constitutional Revolution, had such significance that it was maintained in the personal photo albums of many individuals. Whether the photo was passed from hand to hand while decorated as a postcard with Qazvini's poem or was exported from Quchan to other areas in the form of visit portraits, it communicates the same message as is connoted by Géricault's painting of severed heads.

The Colonel's head was severed to grant him a sacred position. However, both the Colonel and his murderers were granted such positions this time. In her article, Athanassoglou (1992) points out that White Terror era conservatives attempted to depict a supreme role for the executioner and to link him to the king, who enjoyed a sacred position, in order to attribute to the executioner a spiritual trait as the hand of God; therefore, they could justify frequent and abundant executions. A similar condition is also true about

[9] At the time, Mirza Kuchak Khan's head was also cut off of his body once he was killed. No such photo was taken of his head; however, his severed head was displayed for a very long time in Tehran (with a focus on the aforesaid frequently discussed topics in the Iran's political climate).

the Colonel's murderers. Once the Colonel's death occurred and its news was received in Tehran, the Quchani Kurd bigheads, who were previously deemed brigands, proposed their devotion to Qavam ol-saltaneh, the central government, and Ahmad Shah. Accordingly, Sardar Muʿaziz Bujnurdi, their commander, requested official titles and bonuses for participants in the Colonel's murder (Azari 1974; *Iran Daily* 1921). Simultaneously, the sacred position of the Colonel was formed after some time through the decoration of the photo of his head with Qazvini's poems and widespread discontent on the part of intellectuals regarding the Colonel's murder, as expressed in newspapers of the time.

The Colonel's head is reminiscent of a chaotic era in which the contemporary Iranian national identity was formed; the chaos and confusion appeared amidst the central government's conflicts with those who were calling for change and a return to the Constitutional Revolution causes. Colonel Pessiyan, first, in compliance with the central government, attempted to change Khorasan into a part of modern Iran's jurisdiction; however, he was symbolically granted an opposite role when Qavam was released from prison and received the position while he remained in Khorasan. Tavakoli (2008) stresses the Colonel's role during the movement toward modern national unity in such a way that he deems the Colonel's practical measures for reshaping and organizing the army, along with administrative and financial entities in Khorasan, as similar (albeit aborted) actions to what Reza Khan did in the following years. This was how a duality appeared in his early political life: a trait linked to his fate from his presence in Khorasan to the capture and reproduction of the photo of his head. This was a paradoxical trait that, on one hand, depicted him as national hero and, on the other, introduced him as a brigand, nation's enemy, or as equal to such epithets common in the literature of national unity advocates. Thus, this image found its place in the middle of the *inferiority/excellence* semantic duality.

The photo, within the representation of social events, is placed at the point of the coincidence of modernity-associated revolutionary violence and the still-forming memory of national identity. This is a revolutionary violence that is inwardly linked to the *destruction/creation* semantic duality, symbolically realized in the crushing of the Colonel's body, a duality that during Géricault's age was only realized in the body *fragmentation* representation. The Colonel is sacrificed/fragmented so that the audience, via a close look at the photo of his cut-off head, is enabled to understand his ruin as the old antihero symbol in contrast with an upcoming creation.

The picture of the Colonel's head certainly conveys the romantic terror of Géricault's picture of severed heads, with two differences:

First, the horrific scenes of Géricault's works are rooted in the *fashion* of the terror consumption culture in contemporaneous Europe, which to an extent reveals itself in the form of a literary type. However, the Colonel's photo, without any relationship to Persian literature, creates extensive terror in a wide scope when it is exploited as a postcard. It is also interpreted as part of a *picture consumption fashion* in a rather limited scope when it enters personal and family photo albums.

It seems possible now to return the above paragraph that describes the relative match of the fluctuation concept between the two poles of *social sympathy* and *terror honour*, or its placement in the middle of moral growth and decline. The subject who creates the work is not fluctuating between these two poles. On the contrary, the work itself, depending on how it is consumed by society, rolls into one of these poles. And one of these two dimensions is more limited than the other.

Second, Nochlin stresses that romantic terror in the horizontal frame is intensified when contrasted with the axis of beauty and is reliant on the dis-ublimatory characteristic, while the picture of the Colonel's head is vertical in most versions. This feature reminds us of the *inferiority/excellence* conceptual duality. From this viewpoint, another picture of the Colonel's head can be compared to the picture of Robespierre's severed head (Figure 6).

Therefore, the Colonel's head has been led to the same fate as Robespierre's. Robespierre himself was changed from a revolutionary hero to a revolution enemy. However, the emphasis is on the vertical frames of the two cut-off heads, which contrast them with the above image. If one proceeds with Nochlin's argument, the vertical images bring their owners an excellence trait; thus both of these men could be deemed heroes. However, in the above image, by putting the old hero's head beside his murderer – the one who had been previously recognized a brigand – the photographer has attempted to stress the inferiority of the Colonel's position by representing the murderer's victory over the murdered. Therefore, intentionally

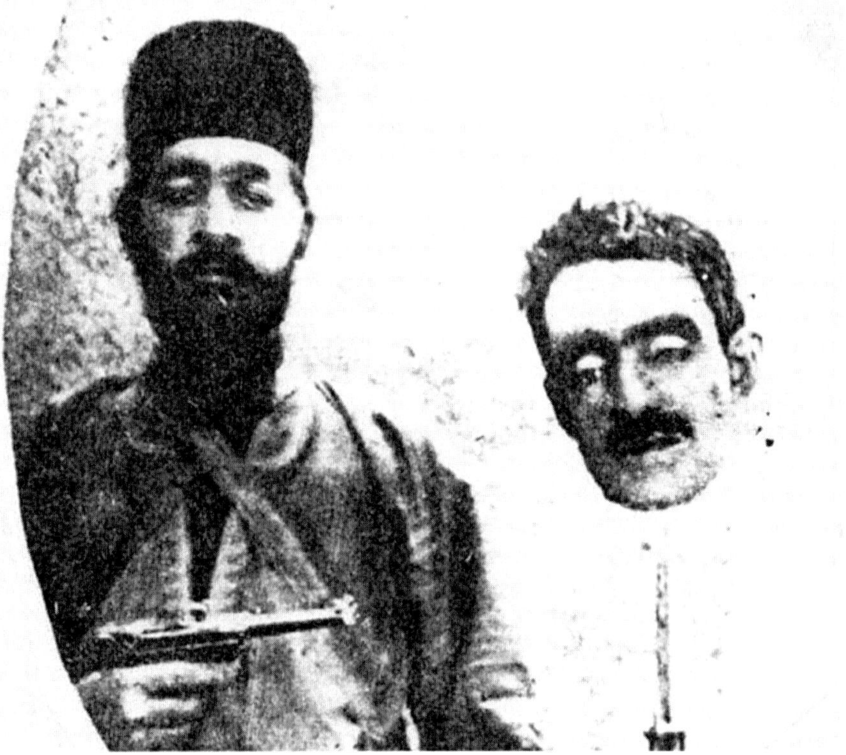

Figure 8: The Colonel's severed head on the bayonet of Farajollah Khan, his murderer

or unintentionally, pleasantly or not, the sacred position of the Colonel was converted into his inferior earthly position.

The Colonel's fate could be perhaps symbolically deemed in contrast to Reza Shah's fate. The Colonel's body in pieces became the metaphor of modernity in Iran. This event occurred at the peak of a chaos period similar to the French episode. The Colonel's head was cut off of his body to be put against the integrated and upright images of Reza Shah, in a conceptual contrast, to comprehend a nation's unity. He sacrificed himself to practically revive the 'disintegration' sense as opposed to 'centralization'. He became an antihero to whom this national identity is indebted in the same way as it is indebted to the struggles of a figure like Reza Khan. What remains of him for us? An image of his head and the survival of this photo are the only signs of his presence among us, and they serve as the material realization of this question in the heart of our history, which is overwhelmed by ups and downs. How did we recognize ourselves as Iranians? Let us take a look at the photo of our heads on our birth certificates.

Bibliography

Abrahamian, E. 2000. *Iran bein-i du Inghilab (Iran between Two Revolutions)*. 3rd. Translated by Kazem Firouzmand, Hassan Shams-Avari and Mohsen Modir-Shaneh-chi. Tehran: Markaz Publication.

Adle, Sh. 2001. 'An introduction to cinema and the first steps in photography and film making in Iran 1899–1907'. *Tavooss Art*, 6 (5).

Afshar, I. 1992. 'Some remarks on the early history of photography in Iran'. In Edmond Bosworth (ed.) *Qajar Iran: Political, Social, and Cultural Change, 1800–1925* Costa Mesa, Calif: Mazda Publishers, 261–291.

Aghaie, K. 2005. 'Religious rituals, social identities, and political relationships in Tehran under Qajar rule: 1850s–1920s'. In Robert Gleave (ed.) *Religion and Society in Qajar Iran*New York: Routledge, 373–92.

Akhoondzadeh, M. 1970. *Dibachiyih tamssilat*. Tehran: Andisheh.

Anon. 2012. 'Russia ii. Iranian-Soviet relations (1917–1991)'. *Encyclopædia Iranica*. http://www.iranicaonline.org/

Anvar, I. 2005. 'Peripheral Taʿziyeh: the transformation of Taʿziyeh from Muharram mourning ritual to secular and comical theatre. *Drama Review* 49 (4): 61–67.

Amanat, A. 1993. 'Russian intrusion into the guarded domain: reflections of Qajar statesman on European expansion'. *Journal of American Oriental Society* 113, no. 1 (Jan.–Mar.): 35–56.

—. 1998. 'Qajar Iran historical overview', In *Royal Iran Paintings, Qajar Epoch* (eds) Layla Diba and Maryam Ekhtiar, 14–28. New York: Tauris and Brooklyn Museum of Art.

—. 2001. 'The Kayanid Crown and Qajar Reclaiming of Royal Authority', Layla Diba (ed.) *Iranian Studies* 34: 17–31.

—. 2008. *Pivot of the Universe*. London: Tauris.

Athanassoglou-Kallmyer, N. 1992. 'Géricault's severed heads and limbs: the politics and aesthetics of the scaffold'. *The Art Bulletin* 74, 4 (December 1992): 599–620.

Azari, S. 1974. *Ghiam-i Colonel Muhaamad Taqi Khan-i Pessiyan (Clonel Pessiyan's upheaval)*. Tehran: NP.

Baktash, M. 1979. 'Taʿziyeh and its philosophy'. In Peter Chelkowski (ed.) *Taʿziya: Ritual and Drama in Iran*. New York: New York University Press, 95–120.

Behdad, A. 2001. 'The powerful art of Qajar photography'. Layla Diba (ed.) *Iranian Studies* 34:141–153.

Becker, H. S. 1974. 'Photography and sociology'. *Studies in the Anthropology of Visual Communication*, 1: 3–26.

Beeman, W. 1981. 'Why do they laugh?: an interactional approach to humor in traditional Iranian improvisatory theater'. *Journal of American Folklore* 49 (374): 506–26.

Beeman, W. and Ghaffari, M. B. 2005. 'Acting styles and actor training in Taʿziyeh'. *Drama Review* 49 (4): 48–60.

Calmard, J. 1996. 'Shiʿi rituals and power II, the consolidation of Safavid Shiʿism: folklore and popular religion'. In Charls Melville (ed.) *Safavid Persia*. London: I.B. Tauris 191–103.

Cezar, M. 1995. *Sanatta Batı'ya Açılış ve Osman Hamdi*. İstanbul: Erol Kerim Aksoy Kültür, Eğitim, Spor ve Sağlık Vakfı Yayını.

Chelkowski, P. 1989. 'Narrative painting and painting recitation in Qajar Iran'. *Muqarnas* 6 : 98–111.

—. 1998. 'Popular arts'. In Layla Diba and Maryam Ekhtiar (eds.), *Royal Iran Paintings, Qajar Epoch*. New York: Tauris and Brooklyn Museum of Art, 90–99.

Chodzko, A. 1878. *Le théâtre Persan, choix de teazies ou drames traduits pour lapremiere fois du Persan*. Paris: H. Paris.

Delrish, B. 1996. *Women in the Qajar Era*. Tehran: Surih Publications.

Demirel, F. 2007. *Dolmabahçe ve Yıldız Saraylarında Son Ziyaretler, Son Ziyafetler*. İstanbul: Doğan Kitap.

Deringil, S. 2002. *İktidarın Sembolleri ve İdeoloji (The Well Protected Domains)*. Istanbul: YKY.

Diba, L.1998. 'Images of Power, Power of Images'. In Layla Diba and Maryam Ekhtiar (eds.), *Royal Iran Paintings, Qajar Epoch*. New York: Tauris and Brooklyn Museum of Art, 30–49.

Durant, W. and Ariel Durant. 2008. *This is a Translation of: The Age of Napoleon*. 2nd Edition, 13th publication. Translated by Esmaiil Dowlat-shahi and Bahram-Beigi Ali-Asghar. Tehran: Elmi-Farhangi Publication.

Eldem, E. 2004. *İftihar ve İmtiyaz. Osmanlı Nişan ve Madalyaları Tarihi*. İstanbul: Osmanlı Bankası Arşiv ve Araştırma Merkezi.

Ekhtiar, M. 1998. 'From workshop and bazaar to academy'. In Layla Diba and

Maryam Ekhtiar (eds.), *Royal Iran Paintings, Qajar Epoch*. New York: Tauris and Brooklyn Museum of Art, 50–65.

Enginün, İ. 2002. *Abdülhak Hamid Tarhan Tiyatroları-5 (Tarık, İbn Musa, Tezer, Nazife, Abdullahü's Sagir)*. İstanbul: Dergah Yayınları.

Etehadiyeh, M.. 1994. 'Women in the Qajar society: the stance of women in the early 19th century'. *Kelk* 55 & 56.

Field, H.. 1964. *Contribution to the Anthropology of Iran*. Persian: translation by Abdullah Faryar. Tehran: Avicenna.

Floor, W. 1999. 'Art and artists in Qajar Iran'. *Muqarnas* 16: 125–54.

Gavin, C. E.S., ed. 1989. *Imperial Self-Portrait: The Ottoman Empire as Revealed in the Sultan Abdul-Hamid II's Photographic Albums, Presented as Gifts to the Library of Congress (1893) and the British Museum (1894): a pictorial selection with catalogue, concordance, indices, and brief essays*. Cambridge: Harvard Semitic Museum *Iran* (newspaper), October 5–7, 1921.

Ghaffary, F. 1984. 'Evolution of rituals and theatre in Iran'. *Iranian Studies* 17 (4): 361–89.

—. 1999. 'Theatrical buildings and performances in Tehran'. In Nikkie Keddie (ed.) *Qajar Iran and the Rise of Reza Khan 1796–1925*. Costa Mesa, CA: Mazda, 94–122

Gobineau, A. 1866. *Les religions et les philosophies dans l'Asie Centrale*. Paris: Librairie Académique.

Hambly, G. R.G. 1968–91. 'Iran during the Reigns of Fath ʿAli Shah' in Avery, In Peter; Hambly, Gavin; Melville, Charles (eds.) *Cambridge History of Iran* Vol 7. Cambridge: Cambridge University Press.

Hedayat, R. 1960. *Rowzatossaffa*. Tehran: Khayam.

Kashani Sabet, F. 'Fragile frontiers: the diminishing domains of Qajar Iran'. In *International Journal of Middle East Studies*, Vol. 29, No. 2: 205–234.

Katouzian, M.H. 2007. *State and Society in Iran, The Eclipse of Qajars and Emergence of the Pahlavis*. 4th. Translated by Hassan Afshar. Tehran: Markaz Publication.

—. 2008. *The Political Economy of Modern Iran, Despotism and Pseudo-modernism*. 14th. Translated by Mohamad-Reza Nafisi and Kambiz Azizi. Tehran: Markaz Publication.

Kaygusuz, B. 2009. 'Poetics and politics of photography'. In *The Representation of Japan in the Photography Collection of Abdulhamit II*. Unpublished M.A. Thesis, Boğaziçi University, İstanbul.

Kazemzadeh, F. 2013. *Russia and Britain in Persia: Imperial Ambitions in Qajar Iran*. London: I.B. Tauris Publishers.

Kirmanshahi, M. 2000. *Maqameolfazl*. Ghom: Allameh Behbahani Institute.

Kürkman, G. 2004. *Osmanlı İmparatorluğu'nda Ermeni Ressamlar 1600–1923*. İstanbul: Matüsalem.

Luft, J.P. 2001. 'The Qajar rock reliefs'. In Layla Diba (ed.) *Iranian Studies* 34: 32–49.

Makdisi, U. 2005. 'Ottoman orientalism'. *American Historical Review* 107, Issue 3: 768–796.

Malekpour, J. 1984. *Adabiyyatih namayishi dar Iran*. Tehran: Tuss.

Marx, K. 1999. *The Eighteenth of Louis Bonaparte*. Translated by Baqer Parham. Tehran: Markaz Publication.

Mascelli, J. 1965. *The Five Cs of Cinematography: Motion Picture Filming Techniques*. Hollywood: Cine/Grafic Publications.

Mechkat, S. 2012. 'Politics of Persian purity: great power rivalry and the emergence of linguistic nationalism in early twentieth century Iran'. *Honours Thesis* Paper 940. Middletown, Connecticut: Wesleyan University. http://wesscholar.wesleyan.edu/etd_hon_theses/940

Mishory, A. 1997. *Théodore Géricault's Grande Suite Anglaise: Sources, Iconography and Significance*. New York: The City University of New York, UMI Microform 9807971.

Mokhlesi, M. A. 1985. *Historical Geography of Soltaniyih, Iran*. Tehran: Jalali.

Mozafar al-Din Shah. 1903. *Safarnamay-i Mubarek-i Shahanshahi*, Tehran, NP.

Nochlin, L. 2001. *The Body in Pieces: The Fragment as a Metaphor of Modernity*. Translated by Majid Akhgar. Tehran: Herfe honarmand.

—. 1994. 'Géricault, or the absence of Women'. *The MIT Press*, 68: 45–59.

Nourbakhsh, H. 1976. *Karim Shirihyi dalqakih mashhurih Nasser al-Din Shah*. Tehran: Sanayi.

Özendes, E. *Abdullah Frères, Osmanlı Sarayının fotoğrafçıları*. İstanbul: Yapı Kredi Kültür Sanat Yayıncılık.

—. 1999. *From Sabah & Joaillier to Foto Sabah: Orientalism in Photography*. İstanbul: YKY.

Öztuncay, B. 2003. *The Photographers of Constantinople: Pioneers, Studios and Artists from 19th-century Istanbul*. Istanbul: Aygaz.

—. 2005. *Khatıra-i uhuvvet: portre fotoğrafların cazibesi 1846–1950*. İstanbul: Aygaz.

—. 2000. *Vassilaki Kargopoulo: Hazret-i Padişahın'nın Serfotoğrafi*. İstanbul: BOS.

Pelly, L. 1879. *The Miracle Play of Hassan and Husain*. London: Allen.

Peterson, S. 1979. 'The Tazieh and related arts'. In In Peter Chelkowski (ed.) *Taʿziya: Ritual and Drama in Iran*. New York: New York University Press, 64–87.

Renda, G. 1992. *Propagating the Imperial Image: Tasvir-i Humayun. Osmanlı padişah portreleri bir 19. yüzyıl albümü: İnan ve Suna Kıraç koleksiyonu (A nineteenth-century album of Ottoman sultans' portraits: İnan and Suna Kıraç collection*. İstanbul, Turkey: İ. Kıraç and S. Kıraç.

Saberi, S. 2008. 'Barrisiyi Tatbighi Qiame Clonel Pessyan va Sheik Mohamad Khiabani (Comparative study of upheaval of Colonel Mohamad Taqi Khan and Sheik-Mohamad Khiabani)'. *Selected Essays in Symposium in study of characteristics and measures taken by Colonel Mohamad Taqi Khan Pessyan*. Tehran.

Sane', M. 1991. *Photography in Shiraz*. Tehran: NP.

Sattari, M. 2003. *Siyrih tahavoli 'akasi*. Tehran: Samt.

Semsar, M. H. 2000. *Golestan Palace Library, A Portfolio of Miniature Paintings and Calligraphy*. Tehran: Zarrin & Simin Books.

Shahidi, A. 2001. *Pajuhishi dar ta'zieh va ta'zieh-khani*. Tehran: Bureau of Cultural Researches.

Sheikh, R. 1999. A critique on anthropological documentary photography on its early years (1840–1900), 'Aksnamih cultural researches office publications.

—. 2007. 'National identity and visual microhistories of the constitutional revolution'. 'Aksnamih cultural researches office publications: 29–44.

—. 2008. Sevruguin and imagery in Iran during late nineteenth century and early twentieth century. 'Aksnameh cultural researches office publications.

Solomon-Godeau, A. 1991. *Photography at the Dock: Essays on Photographic History, Institutions, and Practices*. Minneapolis: University of Minnesota Press.

Soucek, P. 2001. 'Coinage of the Qajars: a system of transition'. Layla Diba (ed.) *Iranian Studies* 34: 52–89.

—. 2000. 'The theory and practice of portraiture in the Persian tradition'. *Muqarnas*, Vol. 17: 97–108.

Stein, D. 1989. 'Three photographic traditions in nineteenth-century Iran'. *Muqarnas* 6: 112–130.

—. 1989. *The Birth of Photography in Iran*. Translated by Ebrahim Hashemi. Tehran: Esparak publications.

Tabatabayi, S. 1984. 'Fatawayih Ulamayih salf darbariyih 'azadari va shabih-khani'. *Honar Quarterly* 4: 290–301.

Tahmasbpour, M. R. 1990. From silver to light, Tarikheh Iran.

—. 2002. *Nasser al-Din Shah, the Photographer*. Tehran: Tarikh-e-Iran publications.

—. 2006. *Italians and Photography in Iran*. Tehran: Ghou publications.

Talayi, P. 2008. 'A survey on women regarding Qajar era'. *Binab quarterly*, Islamic art and culture institute publications, issue 12.

Tarle, E. V. 2008. *Napoleon*. 4th. Translated by Mohamad Qaazi. Tehran: Kharazmi Publications.

Tavakoli, Q. 2008. 'Nezamian va Olgooye Nosazie Amerane dar Iran (Militants and modernization pattern in Iran)'. In *Selected Essays in Symposium in Study of Characteristics and Measures taken by Colonel Mohamad Taqi Khan Pessyan*. Place: Publisher.

Vuurman, C. and Theo Martens. 1999. 'Sevruguin'. In Frederick N. Bohrer (ed.) *Sevruguin and the Iranian Image: Photographs of Iran, 1870–1930*. Washington: Arthur M. Sackler Gallery, Smithsonian Institution; Seattle: University of Washington Press

Yazdi, S. 1941. *Rissayilih Muzafari*. Tehran: Matbaeyeh Shahanshahi.

Yeganeh, C. 2007. 'Modernization and Post-Modernization', 49–107. *1st Symposium of Socialogy of Art*. Tehran: Farhangestan-i Honar.

Zoka, Y. 1997. *History of Photography and Pioneer Photographers in Iran*. Teharn: Elmi Farhangi Publications.

Filmography

Zahedian, M. 2004. *Halqihayih Gumshudih* (Lost Rings), IRIB Channel 4.

Index

ʿArif Qazvini, 119
ʿAshura, 8, 49
ʿakkasbashi, 59, 60, 70, 71
ʿaks, 19
ʿakskhana, 87
ʿAshura, 10
ʿakkasbashi, 68, 70

Abdulah Qajar, 61
Afsharid Dynasty, 89, 91
Agha Reza ʿAkkasbashi, 26, 70
Agha Reza ʿAkkasbashi, 68, 70
Ahmad Shah Qajar, 26
Anglo-Persian Agreement, 80
Antoin Sevruguin, 60, 63, 65, 67–69
Armenian Azerbayjan, 34

Baba Ghuri, 34
Bazi, 9
British military, 80–82
British Pathé, 76
Bujnord, 25, 27
Buyutat-i Saltanati, 87

Constitutional Revolution, 119

Darolfonoon, 5, 61, 87, 96
Dervish, 36
Dezfool, 31

Div, 39

Fath ʿAli Shah Qajar, 89–91, 102, 112
Fatwa, 10, 17, 18
Field, Henry (American anthropologist), 44–46, 143
Firdawsi, 90, 91
First World War (1914–1918), 82
Frances Carlhian, 60

Ghuchan, 36
Golestan Palace, 3, 5, 6, 63, 64, 70, 89, 96–98

Haftlang Bakhtiari, 31
Haram (forbidden), 10
Harem, 12, 48, 63, 64, 100, 105
Hazrat-i Maʿsoumeh, 55
Hazrat-i Maʿsoumeh, 55
Holster, Ernest, 60, 65, 66, 68, 70, 71

Imamzadeh Shah Zayd, 20
Iranian Revolution, 54

Jajerood, 48
Jameʿ Mosque, 53, 55
Jameʿ Mosque, 52, 53, 55
Jew, 44, 45

Kachalak-bazi, 9

Kamalolmolk, 19
Karim the Junkie, 13
Karkhana, 87
Khan, 78, 88
Khaqan, 89
Khaymihshab-bazi, 9
Khurasan, 26, 28
Kirmani, Mirza Reza, 67
Kitabkhan, 87

Luwbat-bazi, 9

Maktab-i Naqqashiy-i Majani, 87
Mandé Louis-Jacques, 59
Mirza Kuchak Khan, 123, 135
Mirzayih Qumi, 17, 18
Montabone, Luigi, 60, 62, 63, 96
Moshir od-Dolih, 123
Mostowfi ol-Mamalik, 78
Mozafar al-Din Shah Qajar, 1, 5–8, 21, 26, 47, 93, 98, 99, 110, 144
Muhammad Taqi Khan Pessiyan, Colonel Pessiyan, 117
Mulla Hadi Sabzivari, 20, 70
Muqalid, 14
Muraqqaʿ, 91
Muʿayirulmulk, 118

Nadir Shah Afshar, 102
Naked, 26, 105
Nakkaşhane, 87
Nanism, 24, 30
Naqqaskhana, 87
Naqsh-i Jahan Square, 55, 56
Nasser al-Din Shah Qajar, 5, 6, 12, 14, 17, 18, 20, 21, 23, 26, 47–49, 60, 62, 64, 67, 87, 89, 90, 94–100, 102, 105, 112
Nasseri Period, 49, 51, 55, 56
Neishabour, 55
Niavaran Palace, 50, 63
Nikoli Pavlov, 60

Orientalist, 59, 72
Ottoman Empire, 97

Pahlavi Era, 53
Pardih-khani, 9
Persian Gulf, 45
Pesce, Luigi, 60, 96
Pope, Arthur Apham, 53
Prince Albert (1819–1861), 81, 82

Qajar era, 8, 9, 11, 52, 53
Qavam ol-saltaneh, 135, 136
Quran, 9, 10, 49, 50, 89

Reza Shah Pahlavi, Reza Khan, 53, 78
Russian cinematography, 78
Russian film, 80–82

Sabzivar, 55
Safavid Era, 54
Sanayi-i Nefise Mektebi, 88
Shabih, 5, 8, 9, 11, 12, 17–19
Shabih-bazi, 9
Shabih-khan, Shabih-khani, 11
Shah Abbas, 56
Shahanshah, Shahanshahnama, 89
Shahnama, 90, 91
Shahr-i farang, 37
Shahristanak, 37
Shiite Imam, 8, 14, 54, 55
Shikh Khazʿal, 124
Slavery, 45
Stevens, George, 60, 62
Surat-khani, 9

Tabriz Arg (citadel), 56
Takkiyih Dawlat, 87, 89
Taq-i Bustan, 91, 102

Taqlid, 5, 8, 9, 14
Tashabuh, 9, 10
Tasuʿa, 49
Taʿzieh, Taʿzieh-khan, 5, 12
Taʿzieh, Taʿzieh-khan, 5, 8, 10
Tehran, 23, 24, 49–51, 61, 65, 96, 118–120, 122, 135, 136, 141–146

Ulama, 100, 112, 115

Vosugh od-Dowlih, 122, 123

Zandieh Period, 56

Iranian Studies

edited by Dr. Pedram Khosronejad (University of St. Andrews)

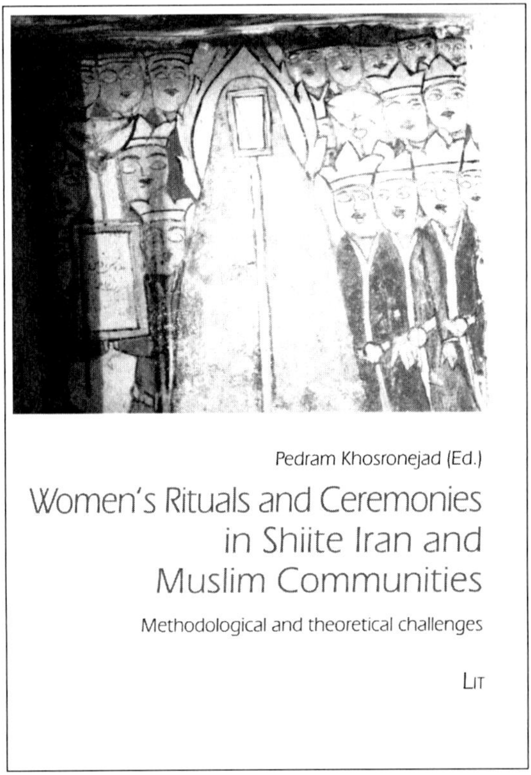

Pedram Khosronejad (Ed.)
Women's Rituals and Ceremonies in Shiite Iran and Muslim Communities
Methodological and theoretical challenges
In this volume the authors present and discuss different aspects of their field research and experience in regard to women's rituals and devotional practices. One of the main aims of this book is to broaden our understanding of women's devotional lives, as well as calling attention to its relation to general social change. Most of the contributions are based on field research, direct observation and participation in rituals. This gives the reader a unique opportunity to better understand methodological challenges related to gender issues and field research among Muslim communities.
Bd. 1, 2014, 152 S., 29,90 €, br., ISBN 978-3-643-90605-2

LIT Verlag Berlin – Münster – Wien – Zürich – London

Auslieferung Deutschland / Österreich / Schweiz: siehe Impressumsseite